Oracle Primavera Contract Management, Business Intelligence Publisher Edition v14

A one-stop reference to concepts and usability of the core modules of a complex application

Stephen D. Kelly

[PACKT] PUBLISHING

enterprise

professional expertise distilled

BIRMINGHAM - MUMBAI

Oracle Primavera Contract Management, Business Intelligence Publisher Edition v14

First published: December 2012

Production Reference: 1041212

Published by Packt Publishing Ltd.
Livery Place
35 Livery Street
Birmingham B3 2PB, UK.

ISBN 978-1-84968-690-7

www.packtpub.com

Cover Image by Asher Wishkerman (wishkerman@hotmail.com)

Credits

Author
Stephen D. Kelly

Reviewers
Daniel L Williams

Deepak Vohra

Bryan Gardner

Acquisition Editor
Rukhsana Khambatta

Lead Technical Editor
Unnati Shah

Technical Editors
Dipesh Panchal

Sharvari Baet

Copy Editor
Alfida Paiva

Project Coordinator
Michelle Quadros

Proofreader
Lawrence A. Herman

Indexer
Hemangini Bari

Graphics
Valentina D'silva

Aditi Gajjar

Production Coordinator
Shantanu Zagade

Cover Work
Shantanu Zagade

About the Author

Stephen D. Kelly graduated from Oregon State University in 1982 with a degree in Construction Engineering Management. He got his start with a mid-sized general contractor who was willing to take a chance with this college graduate and they both saw the benefits of a computer system in the contracting world. Even though the personal computer had not yet come to the scene, Steve was very interested in how computers could help the construction industry to manage time, cost and improve efficiencies. Steve used his knowledge gained at the University and a lot of "on-the-job-training" along with his love for computers to advance in the construction industry. He then moved to computerized estimating and building estimating databases to allow estimators to become more efficient and more accurate. The problem was that the more accurate the estimator became, the more projects he would lose as he was more accurate and not bound to miss anything.

After working for many years in the construction industry in various positions and organizations, Steve decided he wanted to work for many companies at once and help them computerize their business in the construction industry. At this time, Primavera had already placed itself in the forefront of the computerized scheduling market with its DOS product, Primavera Project Planner (P3). Primavera then bought Expedition and started to market this as a project communication and cost controls tool to accompany their flagship product. The rest (as they say) is history.

Steve has been implementing and training with the Primavera suite since 1985. He has worked around the world in many large organizations to help them understand project controls and how to properly implement and use a tool such as Oracle Primavera Contract Management. His company, Pro Management Systems, Inc. has built many third-party applications to enhance the abilities of PCM. Steve has a passion, and is known for his desire to understand a business before even talking about the various tools available. Like he says, "I want to learn how you do business and then figure out how to possibly improve those processes and wrap the tools around them." He relates project management to the fireman profession. He has given speeches on this comparison saying, "Even if a fire is put out quickly, there is always residual damage to deal with." In other words, it is better to keep the fires from starting at all.

He likens that concept to project management and uses the Primavera tools to allow his clients to be proactive rather than reactive. He says, "Why not let the computer tell me what information needs my attention, it is much smarter and faster than I ever dreamed."

Steve has a wonderful, supportive wife of 30 years, five children, and two grandchildren. He lives on a small farm in Oregon where he enjoys time in the out of doors.

I would like to acknowledge that this book would not be possible if it were not for all the wonderful clients I have had the pleasure to work with over the years. University can teach you many things, but book knowledge is not enough in this business. It takes many years of learning from your peers. There are too many to list but you know who you are from the very beginning working with this "greenhorn" college graduate, up through today. Anyone who says he has arrived and knows all about this business is lying. There is so much to learn. I'd like to thank everyone who has had an influence. I cannot leave out my wife Linda and my five children: Dan, John, Kristin, Joe, and David, who have put up with many days, weeks, and months of me travelling around the world while Linda was left home holding down the fort. The most important influence in my life journey is the Lord Jesus Christ. May He get all the glory of all I do.

About the Reviewers

Daniel L Williams first began working with Primavera in 2001 as part of an integration project with JD Edwards World. Since then, he has helped numerous clients integrate Primavera with many other systems, including PeopleSoft, Timberline, and Oracle EBS. His work revolves around helping people make best use of Primavera and other software investments. Sometimes this involves heavy integration; sometimes it involves customization and automation of business processes. Sometimes it simply involves listening to people talk through their business goals and helping them come up with workable solutions. Daniel's background includes a Ph.D. in Physics from Caltech, many years of programming in C, C++, and C#, and for the past decade leading numerous software development projects oriented around Primavera. Dr. Williams is the author of *Oracle Primavera P6 Version 8: Project and Portfolio Management*, *Packt Publishing*.

> I would like to thank my wife, Heather, for being the cornerstone of our family and allowing me to pursue a career I love.

Deepak Vohra is a consultant and a principal member of the `NuBean.com` software company. Deepak is a Sun Certified Java Programmer and Web Component Developer, and has worked in the fields of XML, Java programming, and J2EE for over five years. Deepak is the co-author of the book *Pro XML Development with Java Technology*, *Apress* and was the technical reviewer for the book *WebLogic: The Definitive Guide*, *O'Reilly Media*. Deepak was also the technical reviewer for the book *Ruby Programming for the Absolute Beginner*, *Course Technology PTR*, and the technical editor for the book *Prototype and Scriptaculous in Action*, *Manning Publications*. Deepak is also the author of the books *JDBC 4.0 and Oracle JDeveloper for J2EE Development*, *Packt Publishing*, *Processing XML documents with Oracle JDeveloper 11g*, *Packt Publishing*, and *EJB 3.0 Database Persistence with Oracle Fusion Middleware 11g*, *Packt Publishing*.

Bryan Gardner has more than 15 years of experience in various areas of construction administration, project control, and project management. Prior to joining Critical Business Analysis in 2004, he had managed many projects in the commercial and educational segments of construction. During that time, Bryan gained significant insight into enterprise management systems and information technology for construction. In addition to his years of hands-on experience with Primavera products, in the last eight years, Bryan has consulted for many large and medium size firms for Contract Manager and P6, including clients in the oil and gas, engineering and construction, aviation, manufacturing, and public works sectors.

Bryan is a certified Trainer and Implementation Consultant for Primavera Contract Management and P6. Bryan is proficient in the use of the Oracle BI Publisher and Sybase InfoMaker report writers in conjunction with Primavera products and trains others to be as well.

Bryan has presented on Contract Management topics at the Primavera User Conference in 2007 and 2008 as well as the Collaborate conferences in 2011 and 2012.

Most recently Bryan has been working with the Project Controls group of a major Canadian oil company, working their business functions and specialized reporting requirements into the Primavera application set. Bryan works each day to support the successful implementation and long term use of Contract and Project Management systems, utilizing his real world and consulting experience to provide a sensible and functional solution.

www.PacktPub.com

Support files, eBooks, discount offers and more

You might want to visit www.PacktPub.com for support files and downloads related to your book.

Did you know that Packt offers eBook versions of every book published, with PDF and ePub files available? You can upgrade to the eBook version at www.PacktPub.com and as a print book customer, you are entitled to a discount on the eBook copy. Get in touch with us at service@packtpub.com for more details.

At www.PacktPub.com, you can also read a collection of free technical articles, sign up for a range of free newsletters and receive exclusive discounts and offers on Packt books and eBooks.

PACKTLIB

http://PacktLib.PacktPub.com

Do you need instant solutions to your IT questions? PacktLib is Packt's online digital book library. Here, you can access, read and search across Packt's entire library of books.

Why Subscribe?

- Fully searchable across every book published by Packt
- Copy and paste, print and bookmark content
- On demand and accessible via web browser

Free Access for Packt account holders

If you have an account with Packt at www.PacktPub.com, you can use this to access PacktLib today and view nine entirely free books. Simply use your login credentials for immediate access.

Instant Updates on New Packt Books

Get notified! Find out when new books are published by following @PacktEnterprise on Twitter, or the *Packt Enterprise* Facebook page.

Table of Contents

Preface

For years there has been a call to have a third-party book available for Oracle Primavera Contract Management (PCM). There are many "how-to" books written for Primavera P3-P6, why not for PCM? The problem with writing a "how-to" book for PCM is that the application can be configured in many different ways to accommodate the organization. Scheduling is scheduling; everyone performs that task pretty much the same way. However, there is no one way to manage contracts and therefore no one way to use PCM. Every organization is different and has different processes for each of the 33 available modules within PCM. So, a book cannot be written as a "how to use" PCM for your organization. This book will review the best practice concepts of managing contracts and communication and how to use PCM as a tool to reinforce these concepts. There are several tools available to organizations that provide similar functionality to PCM. They all have their strengths and weaknesses; none of them are perfect. Primavera is the recognized leader in producing applications to manage projects and project related information for several vertical markets. Even though PCM is not perfect, it is the tool against which others are judged. It allows the organization to *own* the data and can be configured for how the organization performs certain business processes.

PCM history

Before we jump into the details, let's look at the history of this application and its humble beginnings. Oracle Primavera Contract Management (PCM) has been around for many years. Primavera has been known as the company of choice around the world for its scheduling tool, but in the beginning very little was known about the product called Expedition. Expedition was acquired by Primavera back in the 1980s as an MS-DOS product. The original product was written around the contract relationship and the Cost Worksheet, although at that time the Cost Worksheet could be overwritten at any time. It was written with a Btrieve® database backend and required a dongle as the security device to make sure you were allowed to use the software. It included most of the modules that are currently available.

Form design at that time was very archaic and required the purchase of a Postscript® printer to properly create the forms.

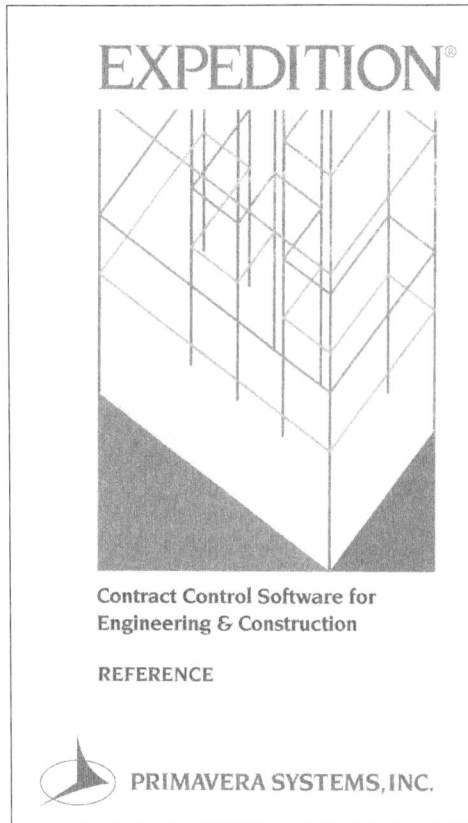

The last version in MS-DOS was v4. As the world was changing and accepting the concept of Windows, Primavera created their first Windows version of Expedition, v5.0. The Windows version allowed multiple registers to be open at the same time. This was good and bad as many users didn't realize this or simply forgot that they had 15-20 windows open at the same time. For those of us who can remember back that far, hardware was trying to keep up with the requirements of Windows and RAM, and hard drive space was expensive compared to today.

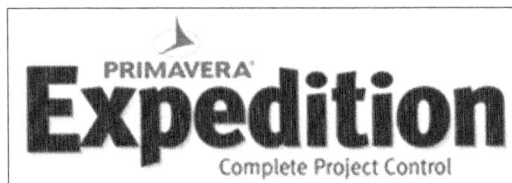

Users loved the multiple open windows concept but each open window used precious hardware resources and often the system was quite sluggish as users forgot that they actually had many windows open at the same time, bringing their machines to a crawl. When Expedition was introduced for Windows, they also moved to a Sybase database and a new Windows-based report writer called Infomaker. Infomaker was a breath of fresh air at the time as it allowed the creation of forms and reports much more easily with its Windows-based interface and the ability to place various object types on the "page" easily, including boxes, lines, data elements, logos, and so on. Sybase was a nice little database engine that could handle large amounts of data with a relatively small footprint.

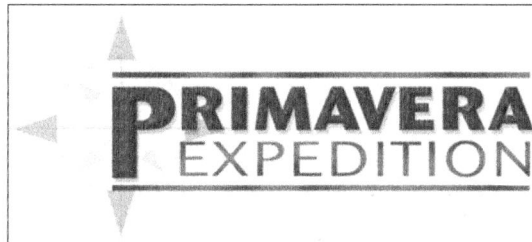

The Windows version of PCM was the version that introduced the Control Center as we know it today. The last version of the Windows product was 8.59. They dabbled in the browser-based application with Version 8.5 by allowing both browser-based and Windows-based clients to be used against the same database on certain modules.

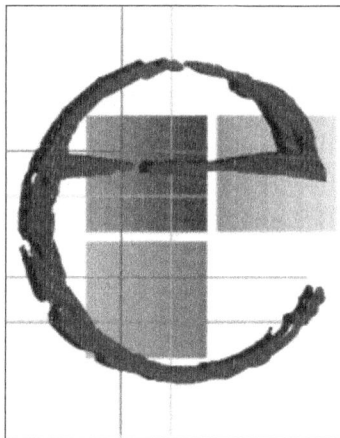

This was a bit of a clumsy time for Expedition as it wasn't exactly clear which client interface to use. When Expedition came out as the first 100 percent browser-based application in this space, it met with very mixed reviews. The first version was a bit clunky and did not include the Payment Certificates module. After a few service packs and releases, it was finally accepted as the latest version of Expedition; or was it? With this version they changed the name to Contract Manager. This would be the first of many name changes to come. Being browser-based meant that there is no application that is loaded on the client machines and there must be a connection to the application server either through the corporate network or through the Internet. The Internet was certainly available; however, bandwidth was nothing like it is today and the concept of fiber was not available. Offices depended on T1 or T3 lines and it was a luxury to have DSL at the remote locations or in your home. As time went on, so were there new features and version of the application. Oracle finalized the purchase of Primavera in January 2010 including all of its applications. With this purchase also came another name change to Oracle Primavera Contract Management. When the acquisition happened there was a lot of speculation as to what would happen to PCM. Oracle then announced the release of two new versions of PCM, one still using Infomaker as its report writing application and the other using Oracle's BI Publisher as the report writing tool. BI Publisher is a much more robust and complete report writing tool but the PCM community initially rebelled against the move since Oracle did not provide a tool or method to convert all the reports from Infomaker to BI Publisher.

PCM versions

Following is a list of all the PCM versions from the beginning and some of the major changes or enhancements with the version:

- **1.x**: Transmittals, Submittals, Correspondence, Meeting Minutes, Requests for Information, Change docs, Purchase Orders, Subcontracts, Deliveries, Bids, Requisitions, Punch List

- **2.x**: Added Issues, Cost Worksheet, Changes, Submittals, and Text file attachments; EGOR text editor

- **3.x**: Multi-user, internal report writer using Postscript printer only

- **4.x**

- **4.2**: Last supported DOS version

- **5.x**: First Windows version including Infomaker report writer; added Dashboard

- **5.1**: Added Requisitions not included in v5.0

- **6.x**: Added Change Management and Drawings; multi-project reports
- **6.3**: Expedition Express added
- **7.x**: Project Center added; use of Microsoft Word as word processor
- **8.x**: Expedition Mobile added
- **8.5**: Some modules available in a browser (RFIs and Safety)
- **8.59**: Last supported Windows version
- **9.x**: First completed browser version
- **10.x**: Procurement Module added; Export to Excel
- **11.x**: Use of Adobe print engine; Microsoft SQL Server database; name changed to Contract Manager
- **11.1**: Can create Change Documents outside of Change Management
- **12.x**: Approval workflow added; E-mail to the Correspondence IN module
- **13.x**: Sybase database dropped
- **13.1**: Last version to use Infomaker report writer
- **14.x**: First version to use BI Publisher for report writing

Quick look at Version 14

PCM Version 14's official name is Oracle Primavera Contract Management Business Publisher Edition. This version has some significant changes to the past versions:

- Sybase database is no longer supported (only Oracle and SQL Server)
- JBOSS webserver is no longer supported (only Oracle WebLogic and IBM WebSphere)
- Infomaker Report Writer is no longer supported (only BI Oracle Publisher)
- Letters module uses BI Publisher instead of Microsoft Word
- New look and feel to match P6
- Oracle Universal Productivity Kit (UPK) available
- Oracle Universal Content Manager (UCM) available

With all the Primavera products, Oracle has leveraged its existing technology into these products. Most of the items listed above existed before the acquisition of Primavera. Oracle has simply added that functionality to these products.

The basic operation and workflow of the application has not changed significantly for several versions. If a user has used PCM back at Version 11 or 12, the basic functionality of that version is still in use today and those users could easily pick up the functionality of this version.

PCM concepts

The basic concept of PCM is as follows:

"Based on security, capture important data related to a project for management decisions, storage, and reporting."

That is basically what PCM does. Based on your user security rights provided by an administrator, you have access to enter data in certain modules where this data can then be reported and flagged for use. This may seem to be a very simple statement and you might be saying "duhhhhh," but the big difference between this type of management and the management of old (prior to computers) is that we are now managing the *data*, and not the *documents*. Prior to computers, the only way to manage a project was to send official contract-related documents back and forth via snail-mail, and when you received a document you made multiple copies of it and placed those copies in various file folders in the file cabinet. For example, if you received a letter from the owner related to a question you had, you would take that letter and make several copies so you could place a copy of that letter into the "Owner Correspondence" file folder, the "Unresolved Issues" file folder, the various folders for each subcontractor involved, and so on. That way when you needed to find a letter that the Owner had written to you, all you had to do was pull the "Owner Correspondence" file and find the one letter you needed amongst the hundreds in the file. Hey, don't laugh; it was better than looking through all the thousands of documents you received over the course of the project.

Today, with the use of computers and databases we can now manage and create both. When we receive the document in any format, we capture the data, and we can then run reports against those data elements as well as "print" a form template that looks great as a document and "send" it to the necessary recipients. One of the many issues I have with the use of spreadsheets in managing project data is that all it does is manage project data; it is quite difficult to take the data elements and then populate a form template with consistency. More about the use of spreadsheets is in *Chapter 4*, *The Almighty Spreadsheet*.

What this book covers

Chapter 1, Welcome to Oracle Primavera Contract Management v14, deals with the basics of a contract and the need for a management tool as well as the different modules included in PCM.

Chapter 2, Information Overload, deals with all the different types of information that needs to be managed on a project and how to classify and store the information.

Chapter 3, So Much to Manage, dives deeper into the types of information on a project and how to register that into PCM.

Chapter 4, The Almighty Spreadsheet, looks at the usage of the spreadsheet as a replacement for a comprehensive tool like PCM; the good, the bad, and the ugly.

Chapter 5, There Is a Better Way, looks at the reasons for needing a tool like PCM to manage and secure all this information.

Chapter 6, The Big Picture, looks at PCM specifically at a high level, the basics behind how it works and how to use it.

Chapter 7, System versus Silo, looks at the differences between the silo approach to management and the system approach and how PCM satisfies the needs of your organization.

Chapter 8, Follow the Money, looks into the details of managing the money side of your project. These are the nuts and bolts of the core of PCM.

Chapter 9, The Only Constant Is Change, looks at the detailed contract change process. You will learn some best practices of setting up the workflow for your organization.

Chapter 10, Time to Get Paid, looks at the payment process in PCM. Getting paid and paying your contractors is important to a successful organization.

Chapter 11, Reading your Crystal Ball, looks at the forecasting process you can use to look into the future on your project.

Chapter 12, Managing Drawings, looks into the management of the drawings or technical documents on your project. Learn how to understand who has which revision of which drawing.

Chapter 13, Processing Submittals, deals with how to properly manage your submittal log rather than just recording history.

Chapter 14, Out in the Field, looks at many of the other modules in PCM usually managed out in the field including RFIs, Meeting Minutes, Daily Reports, and others.

Chapter 15, P6 and PCM, looks at the integration points between these two pillars of the Primavera suite of tools.

Chapter 16, Where Do We Go from Here, teaches you how to get started and properly implement and train PCM to allow your organization to be above your competition.

Chapter 17, The New Contract Management Tool, was added after the announcement that Primavera Unifier is the new direction for contract management using the Skire platform purchased by Oracle in 2012.

Who this book is for

As stated previously, this book will look at best practice concepts of managing contracts and communication, and how to use PCM as a tool to reinforce these concepts. You cannot count on PCM to become your process creator. Processes must be in place before you can use *any* tool to reinforce them. You can't reinforce something that does not exist. Each chapter looks at a project process that needs defining or a concept that is encountered in every organization that is contemplating using a tool to manage project-related information. Each chapter will be very familiar to any organization as a potential issue that will need to be overcome before putting a tool in place. The book is not a step-by-step instruction manual. Every organization is different and a different book would need to be written for each one. This book shows you how to use PCM in situations that affect all organizations that utilize projects. PCM is not just for the construction or engineering world. There are several vertical markets that can utilize these tools. Any organization that places contracts and any user involved in this process can benefit from a tool such as PCM.

PCM has the contractual relationship as the center of the universe. Any organization that places contracts to provide a scope of work can use PCM to manage the monetary aspect of that relationship as well as any communication that happens relating to that relationship. The contractual relationship is the basis for all aspects of PCM. Think of that relationship as the hub of a multi-spoked wheel. All communication and money-related documents or information then come from that hub. Each one of the 32 modules in PCM can be related to, or identified with a contract.

Conventions

In this book, you will find a number of styles of text that distinguish between different kinds of information. Here are some examples of these styles, and an explanation of their meaning.

New terms and **important words** are shown in bold. Words that you see on the screen, in menus or dialog boxes for example, appear in the text like this: "clicking the **Next** button moves you to the next screen."

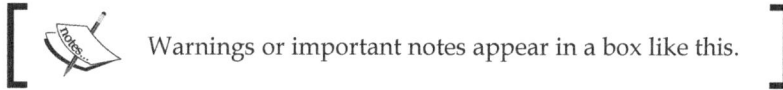

> Warnings or important notes appear in a box like this.

Reader feedback

Feedback from our readers is always welcome. Let us know what you think about this book—what you liked or may have disliked. Reader feedback is important for us to develop titles that you really get the most out of.

To send us general feedback, simply send an e-mail to feedback@packtpub.com, and mention the book title via the subject of your message.

If there is a book that you need and would like to see us publish, please send us a note in the **SUGGEST A TITLE** form on www.packtpub.com or e-mail suggest@packtpub.com.

If there is a topic that you have expertise in and you are interested in either writing or contributing to a book, see our author guide on www.packtpub.com/authors.

Customer support

Now that you are the proud owner of a Packt book, we have a number of things to help you to get the most from your purchase.

Errata

Although we have taken every care to ensure the accuracy of our content, mistakes do happen. If you find a mistake in one of our books—maybe a mistake in the text or the code—we would be grateful if you would report this to us. By doing so, you can save other readers from frustration and help us improve subsequent versions of this book. If you find any errata, please report them by visiting http://www.packtpub.com/support, selecting your book, clicking on the **errata submission form** link, and entering the details of your errata. Once your errata are verified, your submission will be accepted and the errata will be uploaded on our website, or added to any list of existing errata, under the Errata section of that title. Any existing errata can be viewed by selecting your title from http://www.packtpub.com/support.

Piracy

Piracy of copyright material on the Internet is an ongoing problem across all media. At Packt, we take the protection of our copyright and licenses very seriously. If you come across any illegal copies of our works, in any form, on the Internet, please provide us with the location address or website name immediately so that we can pursue a remedy.

Please contact us at copyright@packtpub.com with a link to the suspected pirated material.

We appreciate your help in protecting our authors, and our ability to bring you valuable content.

Questions

You can contact us at questions@packtpub.com if you are having a problem with any aspect of the book, and we will do our best to address it.

1
Welcome to Oracle Primavera Contract Management v14

Oracle Primavera Contract Management is one of Primavera's suite of tools for managing projects. It has been around the industry for over 20 years and has seen many different names; however, the core of the application has stayed the same from the beginning. The design is to manage all aspects of the communication of a project as well as the monetary aspects. As the years have gone by in the construction industry, not much has changed as far as building concepts; we still build things from the ground up. It is tools like PCM that allow us to perform our jobs more efficiently.

This chapter will look into the beginnings of *contracts* and why we need tools like PCM.

Contracts

People have been making agreements between entities ever since there was a need for someone else to perform certain tasks. When an organization determines it needs or wants help with a task, it hires another entity. This can be an individual or a large multibillion-dollar company. When another entity is hired, there is a relationship created in the form of a contract where certain aspects of this relationship are understood. These items can be understood with a handshake or formally documented and agreed upon by the signature of both parties. This list of items can include the following:

- **Scope**: "This is what I want done"
- **Start**: "This is when I want you to start"
- **Duration**: "This is how long I expect it to take once you start"
- **Payment**: "This is how much I'm going to pay you when I am happy with your work"
- **Nonconformance**: "This is what will happen if you do not perform as per the above requirements"

The contract in simplified terms

Let's look at a simplified example. Meet Joe and David. Imagine a caveman named Joe asking his buddy David to make him a wheel; the first question from David was "What is a wheel?"

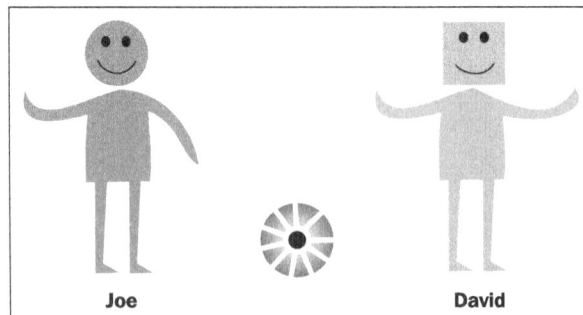

Joe   David

But after all the explanation of how the wheel will revolutionize the world like nothing they have ever seen, they agreed upon the items in the list above. Perhaps the payment was to provide firewood to his family for a year.

The concept of contracts has been around since the beginning of time. Of course at the time of Joe and David there weren't all the sophisticated tools available to manage and track these contracts like there are today. If David did not perform the task of making the wheel on time, was there an understanding of the consequences for this nonperformance? If he provided a wheel with four sides, perhaps the delivery of firewood was delayed or it was not delivered at all.

Now let's expand our example. A cavewoman by the name of Kristin approaches Joe to build a self-propelled chair she has invented.

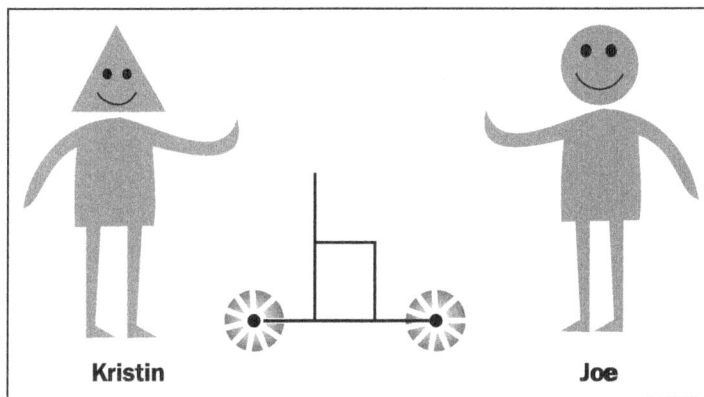

Kristin   **Joe**

After the explanation of how the self-propelled chair will revolutionize the world like nothing else, they discuss all the different parts required to build this self-propelled chair. They come to an agreement with regard to all the items listed above. So Kristin and Joe have now developed a relationship or contract with the items defined. Of course Joe cannot make all the parts required for the self-propelled chair, so he finds other cave people who can produce the chair, frame, and the wheels that were just invented by David. Joe then sends smoke signals to communicate to David to meet about a relationship to produce the wheels for this self-propelled chair. He also contacts a few of his other buddies and places contracts with them to provide the other materials needed.

All the relationships are in place for all the materials required to build this chair.

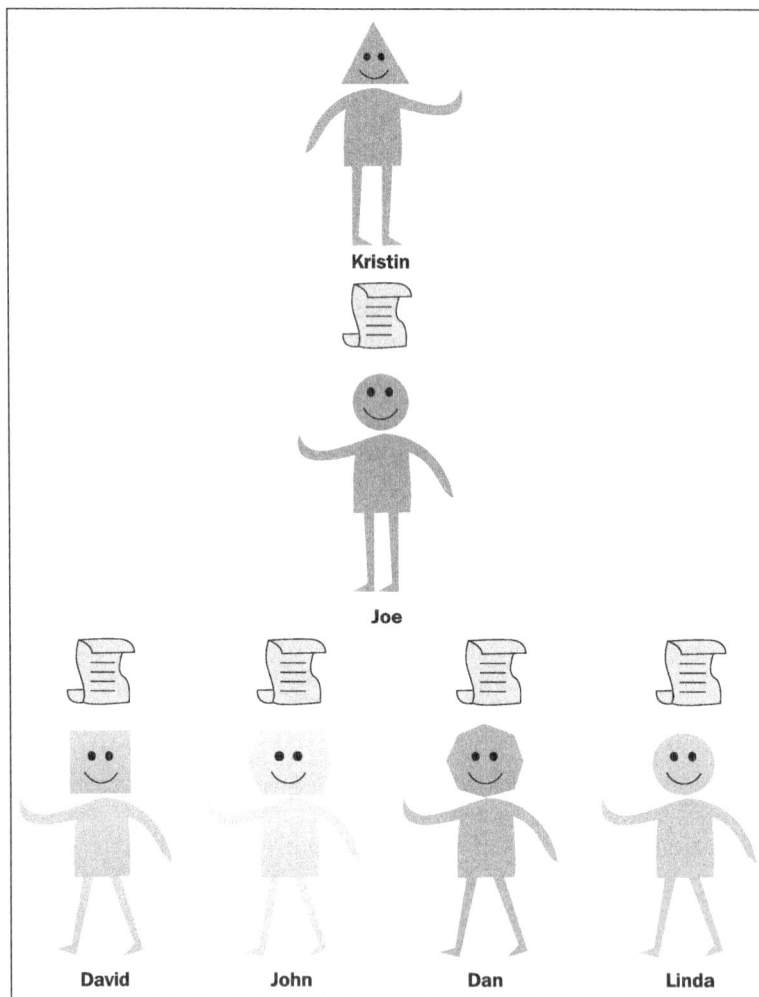

We now have three levels of involvement in building this self-propelled chair; there are contractual relationships formed between each of the levels. Each level will be managing the relationship from their perspective, making sure that the other party in the contract is performing as they had agreed. Each level concentrates on their relationships. David does not care about the relationship Joe has with Kristin; that is Joe's relationship. Joe now has many different contracts in place that he needs to monitor to make sure that the requirements of each contract are being met, either between Kristin and himself or his suppliers of parts and himself. He has many different parties that he will have to communicate with and track these communications just in case David claims that he didn't get paid.

As time progressed, the concept of the contractual relationship became more formalized and the legal profession saw another avenue to make money. So instead of just four or five simple requirements, contracts can be several hundred pages long and many times can only be interpreted by lawyers (perhaps by design – but that is another topic). There is no way that a manager trying to perform a task to fulfill his part of the relationship can understand or even know all the requirements. Enter Contract Management tools like PCM.

What has been described here is a simple form of contract. There are many types of contracts, depending on the type of project and the nature of the industry, with various benefits for one or both parties:

- **Lump sum fixed price contract**: This is the simplest form of contract. The advantage is that both parties know the cost before the project commences (barring any unexpected changes).

- **Unit price contract**: The project is broken into various materials or units with an estimated quantity associated with those units. Payment is made on actual units placed into the project. The advantage is that the customer only pays for what was placed into the project.

- **Many types of cost plus contracts**: The contractor (or service provider) is paid for the costs of what he has put into the project plus a fee based on the percentage. The advantage is that the client only pays for what the service supplier has used on the project plus the agreed fee.

- **Retainer contracts**: This is the typical time and material type of contract. The project is broken into several pieces with a statement of work and an estimate. The client then pays for the materials used and time spent on that scope of work.

- **Incentive contracts**: This type of contract is used typically when there is some uncertainty about the costs of the project. If there are overruns or savings on the project, this is shared between the parties. This minimizes the risk for both.

This is a short list but it shows that there are many types of contracts in which you can engage with another party. PCM can handle any of these types of contracts with a bit of adjustment to some procedures.

Other types of organizations that utilize a tool like this would be organizations that manage a budget bucket of money. This is not a true contract per se; however, it carries all the aspects of a relationship and therefore PCM can be used with these organizations, such as public entities or internal research groups.

Oracle Primavera Contract Management in a nutshell

The contractual relationship is the center of the universe as far as PCM is concerned. There are many aspects to managing contracts in the real world. There is, of course, the monetary aspect of the contract relationship and many other aspects or requirements related to a contractual relationship. Many of these are in the form of *deliverables* - what the contractor will provide to the client These deliverables require communication between the parties of a contract. Being able to understand all these deliverables and requirements, and when they need to be delivered, can be a daunting task. All these deliverables and requirements are tracked in PCM. All the modules within PCM are linked to a contract relationship and therefore allow monitoring of this information at the contract level.

Here is a list of the out-of-the-box modules provided in PCM. They are broken down by a folder structure, as follows (the module tree is configurable so your tree may be different):

Project Information
- Companies
- Issies
- Schedule (link to P6 - see *Chapter 15, P6 and PCM*)

Communication
- Request for Information (RFI)
- Notices
- Noncompliance Notice
- Correspondence Sent
- Correspondence Received
- Transmittals
- Letters
- Meeting Minutes
- Telephone Records
- Safety
- Notepads

☐ Contract Information
 ◦ Cost Worksheet
 ◦ Contracts – Budget
 ◦ Contracts – Committed
 ◦ Contracts – Funding
 ◦ Purchase Orders
 ◦ Trends
 ◦ Payment Requisitions
 ◦ Change Management
 ◦ Proposals
 ◦ Change Orders
 ◦ Procurement
☐ Logs
 ◦ Drawing Sets
 ◦ Drawings
 ◦ Submittal Packages
 ◦ Submittals
 ◦ Materials
 ◦ Daily Reports
 ◦ Insurance
 ◦ Punch List

There are a total of 33 modules available today and five of those modules allow for unlimited document types or acronyms: Notices, Noncompliance, Requests, Proposals, and Changes. Within each of these modules, an unlimited number of that document type(s) are allowed. These modules are available at the project level. When a project is created, it automatically has all these modules associated with that project.

Regardless of the type of business you have (IT, Infrastructure, DOD, Contracting, and so on) or the various types of communication you currently use, PCM can accommodate them. It does not matter what level of the project hierarchy you occupy, the one represented by Joe, David, or Kristin; since all levels manage the contractual relationship, all levels can use PCM for their organization from their perspective. PCM allows using your specific acronyms and document types. The text within the system can also be configured to match your terminology. Many systems force your company in their box and make you change your terminology to match theirs.

Every document in every module can be associated with a specific contractual relationship entered in the system. This allows for all contract-related communication to be assembled and reported.

Don't be afraid

Many organizations think that implementing a tool like PCM is like throwing Microsoft Word on your desktop and telling you to use it. We all know that 90 percent of us only use about 10 percent of MS Word. Tools such as this are a discipline product; if you have the discipline to correctly use it, it can do great things. PCM is a way of life type product; your organization will come to depend on it to manage each set of contracts. PCM requires some forethought and planning before it can be used in an organization. There are many questions that need to be answered to properly set up this powerful tool. Often, those questions do not have ready or immediate answers; implementing a tool like PCM will force organizations to provide those answers. This is not a bad concept; don't be afraid. This exercise will help your organization mature and become better informed about project information and contract management. There is so much information that needs to be tracked and managed, that there must be procedures in place to make sure that nothing slips through the cracks. PCM will also shine a light on items that currently are in the dark, either intentionally or not. It is a tool that forces accountability within the project team. This is why many users are afraid to implement a tool such as this. PCM will expose those areas that are typically lacking in your organization. Every organization is different as to what those areas are and the effects of exposing them.

Change in an organization can be extremely hard. This is not something you didn't already know. Most managers and/or their subordinates do not like change. They have become very comfortable with the status quo. They have their very special spreadsheet that they can manipulate to show upper management. Many say, "Since the current system works, why do we have to change?" We need to define the word "works" in that question. All may be fine with the project manager and everything works for him, but for upper management, all is not fine. They have been wondering why, even though the project manager tells them all is great until the end of the project comes, the profit margin is not what they had expected and been told for the duration of the project. Many times upper management say, "If we had only known about those issues before the end of the project." PCM allows the upper management to have a view into the projects if required. It offers real-time information for reporting. They can run these reports any time from their control center. From the perspective of the enterprise, graphically they can see how aspects of the project are going. The following screenshot shows the **Control Center** screen of PCM:

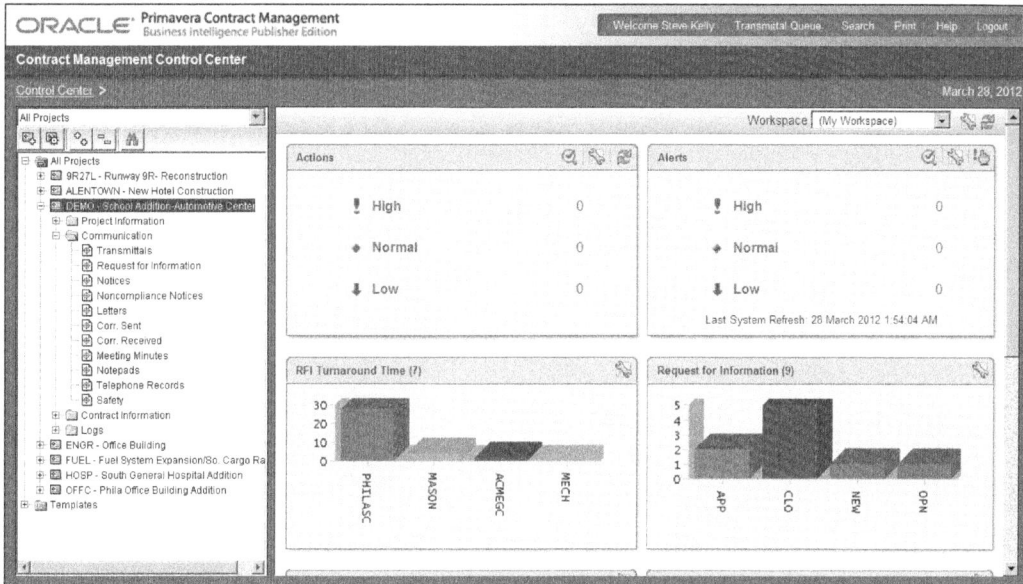

The health of a project can be visible from the Control Center of PCM. By reviewing the graphs available and the alerts that affect your position, you can concentrate your time where it is needed and make proper decisions for the project.

Summary

Oracle Primavera Contract Management application is the tool that other applications are measured against. In terms of projects, it invented the class of Contract Management software and has remained an innovative leader in that category. The latest version (version 14) provides an easy to use, robust database architecture that allows management of all levels throughout an organization to understand all aspects of their project in real time. They then can use this information to make informed and timely decisions.

With the many types of contracts available and the multiple projects being managed at the same time, a computerized tool to help in the management of this information is critical to efficient project management.

In the next chapter you will be exposed to the vast amounts of information available to a project and how to start organizing it for your benefit.

2

Information Overload

The world has changed significantly from the days of Joe and David with regards to the types and delivery methods of information. Information is king and some people just can't get enough of it. With the advent of the World Wide Web, there are literally unlimited sources of information. When we don't know where to find information, we just "Google it." In January 2011, Google's index was approximately 15 billion web pages; by the end of the same year it had grown to almost 50 billion (http://www.worldwidewebsize.com/).

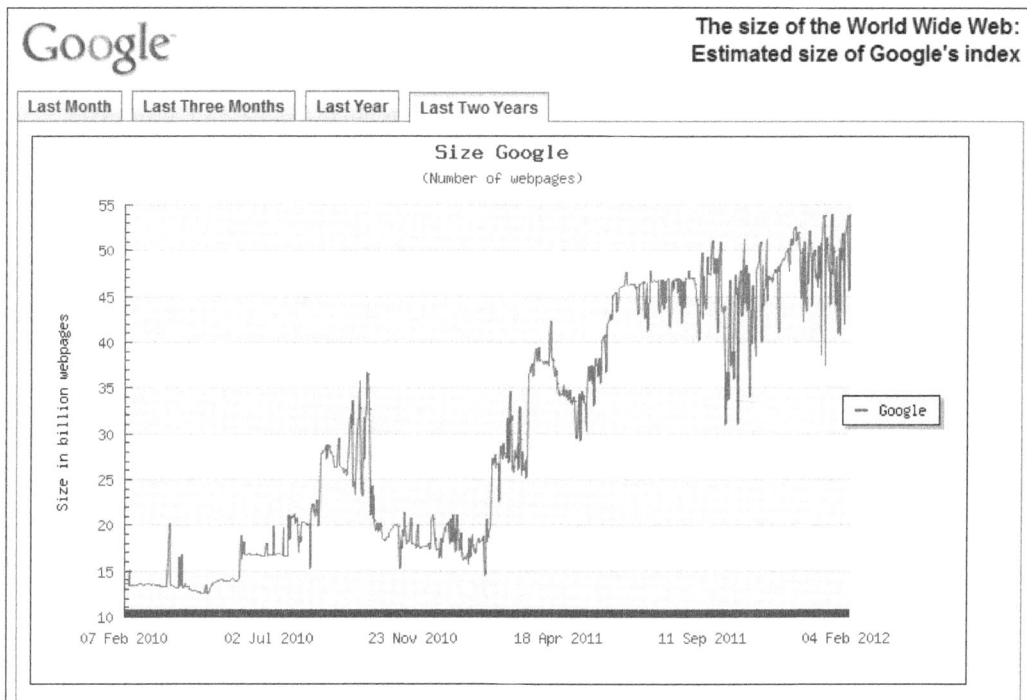

No matter how we look at it, that is a lot of web pages. Finding the relevant information is the key to managing your project. Google claims it can search for keywords in tenths or hundredths of a second. At the top of each search, Google brags about how many hits it found and how long it took to find them.

On your project, finding the information that is relevant to you and needs your attention is the key to any management system, and your success.

Types of project information

There is not enough space on these pages to list or explain the many types of information relating to a project. Some of these include a master contract, a task order relating to that master contract, a notice to proceed that allows the contractor to proceed while he or she waits for an official change order, notification documents that are official notices of an upcoming or past due event, and many more. Each of these documents provides an opportunity to record a date on which responses must be given or completion of the action must be taken. With this information, we can report on upcoming tasks that need our attention. Organizations use different acronyms and names for all the different types of documents. Every organization has its own language when talking about documents or information. When you see the word "budget" or "claim", you understand exactly what is meant by that term—or do you? You know what the term means to you and your organization, but do you know that other organizations see those terms through differently colored glasses? Those terms may mean something slightly or completely different. In some cases the term means the opposite of what you think. PCM allows you to change the terminology to match your organization so when a term is used in conversation or it is seen in PCM, it means the same thing.

PCM allows the organization to use its acronyms when defining all the different types of documents used for a project. The following screenshot shows a subset of the different acronyms and document types that are available out of the box when PCM is installed:

Document Setup   help

	Add Document Type	Add Reference Type			
☑	LOT	Transmittal	Transmittals	LOT	Transmittal
☑	LTR	Letter	Correspondence Letters	LTR	Letter
☑	MAIL	E-Mail			Reference Type
☑	MAT	Delivery Tickets	Material Delivery	MAT	Delivery Tickets
☑	MBI	Meeting Business Item	Meeting Minutes	MBI	Meeting Business Item
☑	MTG	Meeting Minutes	Meeting Minutes	MTG	Meeting Minutes
☑	NCN	Noncompliance Notice	Noncompliance Notice	NCN	Noncompliance Notice
☑	P3	Schedule	Schedule	P3	Schedule
☑	P3R	P3 Resources	P3 Resources	P3R	P3 Resources
☑	PAD	Notepad Item	Notepads	PAD	Notepad Item
☑	PADN	Notepad	Notepads	PADN	Notepad
☑	PAI	Procurement Alternate	Procurement	PAI	Procurement Alternate
☑	PAIB	Procurement Alternate Bid	Procurement	PAIB	Procurement Alternate Bid
☑	PC	Procurement Company	Procurement	PC	Procurement Company

Close

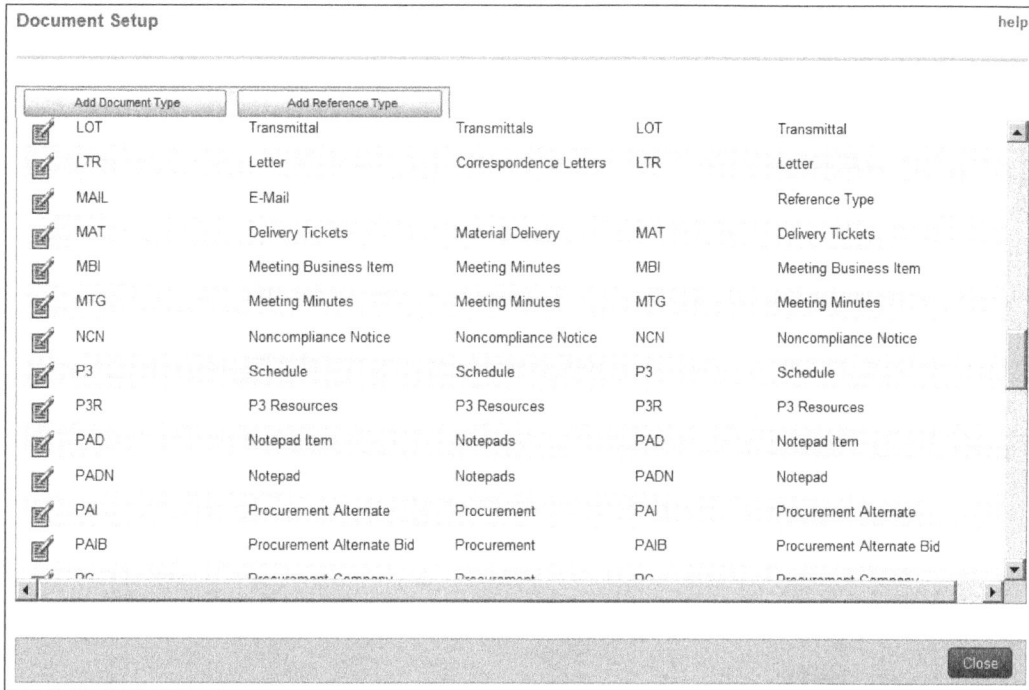

The **Document Setup** function lets the administrator define document acronyms to be available for use in your organization. This lets the system mirror your organization rather than a system where the organization needs to interpret what the system means. These acronyms can be used for information types sent out from the organization or all the different types of documents received by a project from outside parties. Being able to apply a document type to all documents received in or sent out from a project is the first level of organizing the data, that is, by document type.

For example, a document that a contractor sends out to its subcontractors requesting a price for a change in scope can be called several different things. It can be a Request for Proposal (RFP), it can be a Request for Quotation (RFQ), or it can be a Change Order Request (COR). Each organization needs to define each of these document types and standardize them. Your organization wants *one* document for a process and not to have every project manager call the example above whatever they want.

There must be a standard set by the organization as to what terms or *language* will be used within the organization.

> This language is not to be confused with the different foreign languages available in PCM. The language spoken of here are the terms used by an organization to mean certain things.

When an organization contracts with another organization, there must be a meeting of the minds as to the *language* that will be spoken for the project. This many times ends up being a combination of the two organizations, but for a project to go smoothly all parties related to that project must speak the same language.

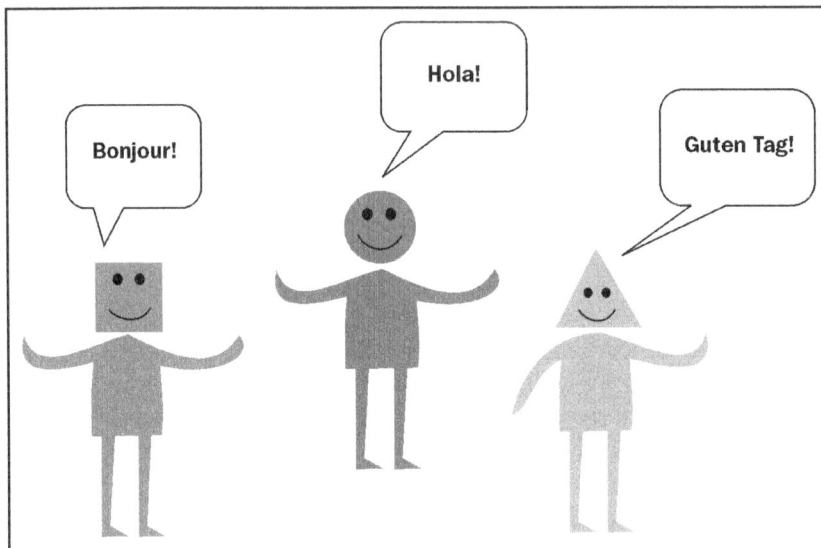

There are many places within PCM where a dictionary is used to help describe a document type or give it attributes that describe the document. Be careful when using these dictionaries as some of them are project specific while others are group specific.

This first level of document organization in many cases uses the modules within PCM as the repository for storage and retrieval of the documents. Each module in PCM has different attributes that provide the uniqueness of the document type or related types.

Understanding the document types and how they fit into the modules within PCM is the start to properly setting up PCM for your organization. You must become familiar with the different attributes of each module and be able to best relate those attributes to the attributes required of each document type. Each module has its own set of unique characteristics.

Customized text is available to change the text of the data entry field names as well as the tabs, error messages, and many other places. This will change the text for all projects, so this is organizational text versus project text. You must be careful with this functionality as well. When you change the word `Date`, it may change in places you did not expect.

Where does all this information come from

No matter the size or type of your project, information is coming in fast and furious. All aspects of a project require capturing data from documents for later retrieval, analysis, or distribution to other parties. An organization must have a platform in place to properly capture and manage all this information.

This information can come from all kinds of sources, such as:

- Clients
- Contractors
- Public
- Owners
- Engineers
- Architects
- Internal parties

And this information can be delivered by many different methods, such as:

- Hand delivery
- Mail (snail-mail)
- Courier
- E-mail
- FTP site
- Collaboration site
- Website
- Cloud storage

There must be a proper flow of this information, whether it is a document that is being received by the project or a document that is being sent from the project. Either direction requires proper procedures to be followed to make sure the proper data is captured and the information ends up in the correct hands for analysis and possible action.

A document flow or distribution matrix must be set up to ensure that all types of information are assigned the correct distribution and actions among the project team. It is not the responsibility of the Document Controller to properly distribute any documents unless they have this matrix available to them. Their role is to facilitate the flow of the documents based on this matrix, not to try and guess who needs to see what document.

Sample Distribution Matrix					
Document Type	Project Manager	Cost Manager	Project Engineer	Quantity Surveyor	Document Control
Correspondence Letter	X				X
Answer to RFI			X		X
Change Order Request	X	X			X
Payment Application	X	X		X	X

Each of the documents above follows a document received workflow with PCM being an integral part of managing this information. Many times responses to these documents must happen within a certain timeframe declared in the contract.

There are so many terms thrown around these days related to the management of documents and proper storage and retrieval. Here are just a few of the terms that have come into use with the advent of the Internet and document storage: document management, correspondence, collaboration, repository, metadata, fields, records, query, the cloud, iDrive, and more. The key to any document management system is the storage, retrieval, and management of the document. At any point in time you should be able to review the history of any document to see who has seen it and on what date(s). You should be able to know when a certain action must be taken on a document before there are consequences to the project. There is a wide variety of types of communication within a project. Imagine if you are running multiple projects with all these types of communication; there is no way you can keep track of all the issues and responses required to keep up with the project.

PCM is not designed as a true document management system with check-in/check-out, proper version control and document history. Therefore if your organization requires such a system, it is best to use another system or repository for proper document management and then link the records back to PCM.

Using a hierarchical structure

Computerized systems allow us to easily incorporate a hierarchical structure in our projects as well as information within these projects. PCM allows for multiple hierarchies that can be easily switched. Hierarchical structures allow us to organize our projects at different levels. They also allow us to provide roll-up reporting at the various levels. Look at the following hierarchical structure:

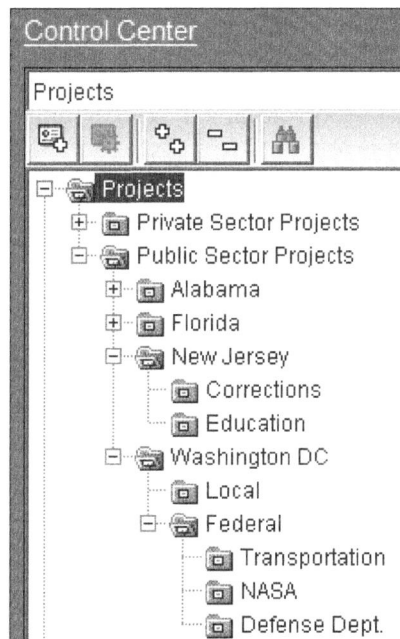

You can see that security would be important at the various levels of the structure. You would not want users who have access to the **Private Sector Projects** to have the same access to the Federal defense projects. Security is assigned at the project level, but the hierarchical structure can give us a visual look at the different levels. When PCM is used in conjunction with Oracle's Primavera Project Management tool (P6), it is good practice to match the hierarchical structure within PCM to that of P6 and the Enterprise Project Structure (EPS).

You can also see that roll-up reporting is very helpful. Every hierarchical node in the structure can provide a roll-up report of all projects at and below that node where the user has permissions. So you can run a report of all projects at NASA as well as a report of all federal projects.

PCM allows for up to ten different hierarchical structures so you can slice and dice your projects and organize them in many different ways. An idea of a structure would be as follows:

- Project type
- Region or location
- Project manager (personnel)
- Local office

Each of these types can be broken down into unlimited subgroups within the hierarchy. Changing views is as simple as selecting the view from the drop-down list at the top of the tree. All your projects will be rearranged and organized by a different structure. A project is assigned to a node (or nodes) on the tree. A project can be assigned to multiple nodes so roll-up reporting at each node can have the proper information. Determining where the project fits in your hierarchical structure is key to a good implementation. Some information has project-level ramifications while others have database or group-level ramifications. This helps determine where your project fits. "What defines a project for my organization?" The answer to this question is determined by several factors. The following are a few factors to consider::

- How will the costs be rolled up?
- How will the funding sources be managed (one or multiple)?
- How will the documents be managed?
- How will the contracts and POs be managed?

Understanding the hierarchy of your organization and where the project fits in that hierarchy allows for better understanding of document flow and roll up of information. More on this in *Chapter 6, The Big Picture*.

Storage of information

There is a vast amount of information used and stored on a project; everyone knows this. It is how we use that information that sets us apart. Information is received at a project in many different formats. An information management system needs the ability to accept this information in its native form and be able to manage the data in the form to be used by the different parties on the project. This is not a job for the all-powerful spreadsheet (see *Chapter 4, The Almighty Spreadsheet*). The system must incorporate security, accountability, and storage so that all parties that need access to this information can have it in real time from anywhere in the world.

PCM utilizes a network (intranet or Internet), a browser, a secure database back-end, and a search engine to allow users quick and easy access to the information that is relevant to them: the network to be able to access the information from anywhere; the browser for the easy-to-use, familiar interface; the security of the database to restrict information from users as required; and a database to store the data fields in a tabular structure for easy search and retrieval of information.

There are several methods that PCM allows the organization to to store external documents or attachments. Since the search engine within PCM does not allow for robust searching inside of attachments, Oracle has provided options for this functionality. There are three methods for storing external attachments, as follows:

1. **Server file storage**: The attachments will be stored in a directory that the administrator selects for each project. This can be, (and is recommended), as a location that is not accessible to the users.

2. **SharePoint**: For those organizations that already use SharePoint in one way or another, PCM allows connection to a SharePoint site with the attachment files stored there. This allows for accessibility from the SharePoint side with SharePoint security.

3. **Oracle Universal Content Management**: Attachments will be stored in the Oracle content repository. This also allows for accessibility from the repository side.

Any of these methods will store externally attached files in a secure location. You must be sure to apply some security to any of these methods to protect the one version of the truth from within PCM.

As stated before, there needs to be a determined document flow and distribution matrix for each project. PCM can then be used to manage the information and notify the proper parties of items that need their attention. PCM records the initial receipt date of a document and then the distribution of that document to various parties. Dates are entered that tell the parties involved when a response or action needs to take place. All this information is used across all documents in one or multiple projects to inform the users of the documents that they need to concentrate on, and allow them to be proactive in getting these items accomplished.

There are many ways to store information; this aspect is typically not the element that hinders the project control aspect of a successful project. It is how the information is used. It is the use of an application on a computer to analyze the data quickly and without bias to help determine what specific information the users should be concentrating on. This allows for efficient use of time, telling the user about items that are about to come due before it is too late.

You might wonder why in the world we have to store every little bit of communication on this project. If you are ever involved in a claim or dispute, then having all this information will be in your favor. In litigation cases, the largest and most organized pile of paper wins; PCM provides a very large and very organized pile of electronic paper with search capabilities. This project information can be held in a database for a long time. PCM allows for the concept of archiving, which is to pull closed projects off of the active database but still have them available to review data. Security can be placed on these archived projects that limit the access to "view only."

Summary

Information is king in this society; however, if you don't know how to manage this information or use it to your benefit, it becomes your enemy. Usually an organization does not understand this concept until it has been engaged in some sort of litigation where if it had properly managed the documents and information it would have saved a lot of time, money, and headaches.

In the next chapter we will look at all the different types of information in more detail. We will see how they can all be related and stored in PCM.

3
So Much to Manage

With all this information and critical decisions being made based on this information, there must be an organized way to store and manage it. It is not as simple as placing all the documents into a folder structure on the F:\ drive. There are many different types of documents that require different responses, security, and accountability. You can't treat a simple bulletin as you would a change order or contract. The change order has monetary and legal ramifications. If for some reason it slipped through the cracks it would potentially have much more impact against the project than a bulletin. When information comes into a project, the type of document must be determined to follow the proper workflow for storage and action. There is a set list of modules within PCM, which can be configured for the organization to hold and manage the various documents.

Types of information

Communication on a project needs to be reviewed from many perspectives. Many people look at PCM as simply a template creation tool. It is so much more than that. To see these benefits we need to analyze the information related to a project. Let's look at project communication in the following way:

- Data elements (metadata)
- Document template (collection of data elements placed on a form)
- Supporting information (attachment files)

The data elements are the fields of information that are captured for management, analysis, and reporting purposes. These elements can be captured from information received into your organization for a project or information being sent from your organization regarding a project. PCM organizes this information into one of the many modules. Each module within PCM is designed with specific requirements and business rules in mind. Following are examples of types of data elements that are used by these modules:

- Date received
- Date response is required
- Who is responsible
- Title
- Notes or remarks
- Monetary information
- Specific query or question
- Impact to project

The actual document or template is in the printed form or PDF of the metadata in a professional, organized, and understandable output. Following is an example of such a printout using the data entered into the fields of the RFI module in PCM:

This part of the communication is important for the receiving party to understand what may be required as a result of this communication. Consistency of this output is required for a consistent method of communication for the organization. Many organizations do not require a consistent method of communication but allow project managers to create their own methods. This method of management does not portray a consistent, organized methodology for project communication within their organization. In a perfect world, I suppose, there would be no need for printed or PDF templates as all the parties would have their own access to the data and be able to approve or comment on the data online. This would be the utopian world of collaboration where all parties access the same data and live happily ever after. To date I have not seen a tool where this is effectively accomplished; true collaboration for the most part is a myth in this author's opinion, as every party is looking out for their best interests. There are many books and articles written on the subject of collaboration. Looking at the output from a project, these are some of the forms that can be produced.

- Contract
- Purchase Order
- Request for Information
- Notice of Noncompliance
- Memo
- Request for Proposal
- Change Order
- Requisition for Payment

These are just a few of the different types of templates that would be sent or received on a project. Included with these templates may be supporting information such as drawings, spreadsheets, pictures, and others that need to be attached to that record. These would be the supporting documents to the record that holds the data fields.

Since PCM was designed with the construction project in mind, these modules are designed for construction related documents. However, PCM has also been configured for other vertical markets and types of organizations. If your organization is deciding whether to use PCM and is not construction related, do not just throw out this tool as an option. There are many non-construction related organizations that use PCM successfully such as IT, finance, research, and many others.

Information sent or received

Information is broken down into two main workflows: information sent from the project and information received by the project. Usually this information is sent or received in the form of a document that explains who the information is from and who the information is meant for. It is typically some sort of formalized template. Many times the same document is received into the project; it is analyzed, approved, marked up or reviewed, and then sent from the project.

Information sent

For the system to be complete, all project related information must be communicated or at least recorded through PCM. Let me say that again: all project related information must be communicated through PCM. If this best practice rule is broken, the concept of a system to hold all project related information is gone. One of the main concepts in using a system like PCM is to capture, manage, and report on any information within the project. If information is communicated in any other way, it goes to reason that all the project information is not in the same place. The biggest offender of this rule is e-mail. The reason we use e-mail so much is that it is easy and quick to use. The reason it is the worst form of communication when related to a project is it is easy and quick to use. Unless there is some mechanism to allow e-mails to be properly captured, leave e-mails to asking about the big game over the weekend. Sadly, most of the time that last statement falls on deaf ears. The following section explains how PCM can help alleviate this problem by using a project e-mail address.

With the understanding that any information that needs to be communicated should be placed in PCM and then delivered to the other party, it is perfectly fine to use e-mail as a transportation vehicle for this information. That means the information would be an attachment to the e-mail. The information (metadata) is entered into the fields of the proper module and when it is time to communicate with the receiving party you can print the template or create a PDF for e-mailing. Less and less templates require a wet signature, so creating a PDF for e-mailing is becoming the most widely used form of communication on a project.

Information received

All project related information received to the project needs to be recorded as received. In PCM this would be using the **Correspondence Received** module. This way, information regarding the time and date the information was received can be tracked. Once it is received into the system, the decision needs to be made as to whether the data on the communication needs to be entered into one of the modules in PCM. An example would be a response to an RFP (Request for Proposal).

The response is received and entered into the Correspondence Received module by recording the date and time it was received and so on. This type of document, of course, needs to be entered into PCM as a response to a Request in the Change Management module with the actual data elements being captured. An example of not needing to record the data elements would be if the contractor sent a revised copy of his schedule to the project. You must record that the schedule was received with a time and date but there is no place in PCM to enter schedule information (unless you are managing the schedule as a submittal). There is also a difference between formal communication and informal communication. Most companies are very specific as to what formal communication really is for a project. More and more companies are creating a project e-mail address and referencing that in their contracts for the contractor to use for formal communication. PCM can recognize one e-mail address per project that can act as the project e-mail address. If e-mails are sent to that project e-mail address PCM will receive it to the **Correspondence Received** module including any attachments to that e-mail. This allows for a project e-mail address to be captured in the structure of PCM. However, that is as far as PCM will take the e-mail. There needs to be a role that monitors this module for e-mails and routes the communication to the proper person.

If you understand these concepts stated in the previous paragraphs you are way ahead of most users of any type of system such as PCM. To summarize, all data being sent from the project needs to be entered into a module in PCM and then the template or form needs to be delivered to the proper parties. All communication received into a project needs to be recorded as received with a time and date and then perhaps the data elements need to be captured for management and reporting by placing that information into one of the OPC modules.

Module Types

There are many types of modules in PCM. The following are module types where multiple document types (acronyms) are allowed and will help you understand these types and how they are used:

- Request Documents
- Notice Documents
- Noncompliance Documents
- Proposal Documents
- Changes Documents

Each of these document types has its own set of attributes. Each of them can also have an unlimited number of document acronyms assigned for an organization. The following section provides a more detailed look at each of these document types.

Requests

The Request module is designed for question and answers. If there is a request for information this module is the official mechanism to ask that question. This module can also be assigned security for determining who gets to ask the question and who should answer the question. The following screenshot shows how the **Question** tab of the Request module is laid out and some of the data elements. The tabs are used to hold different data elements.

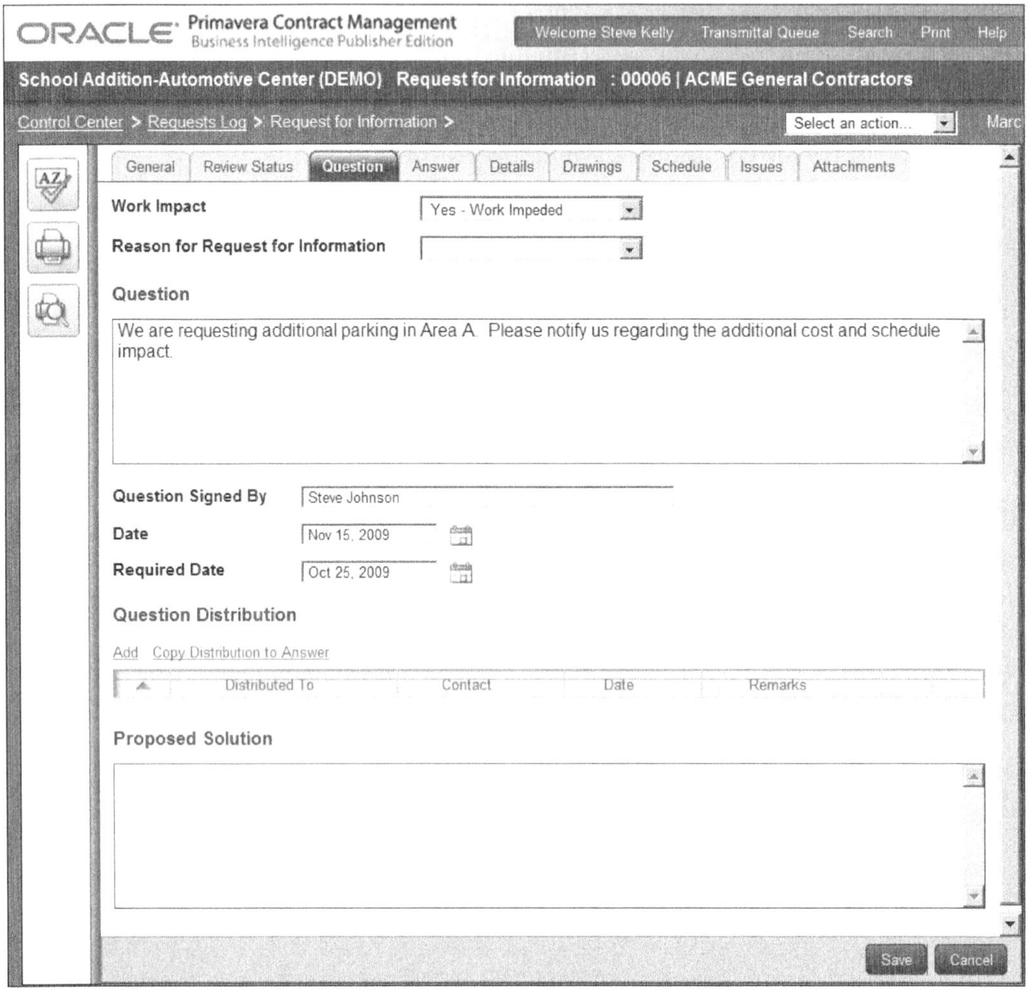

The answer to the request is placed in the same record to keep all the pertinent information about the request in the same document. The following screenshot shows the **Answer** tab and the data elements stored on this tab:

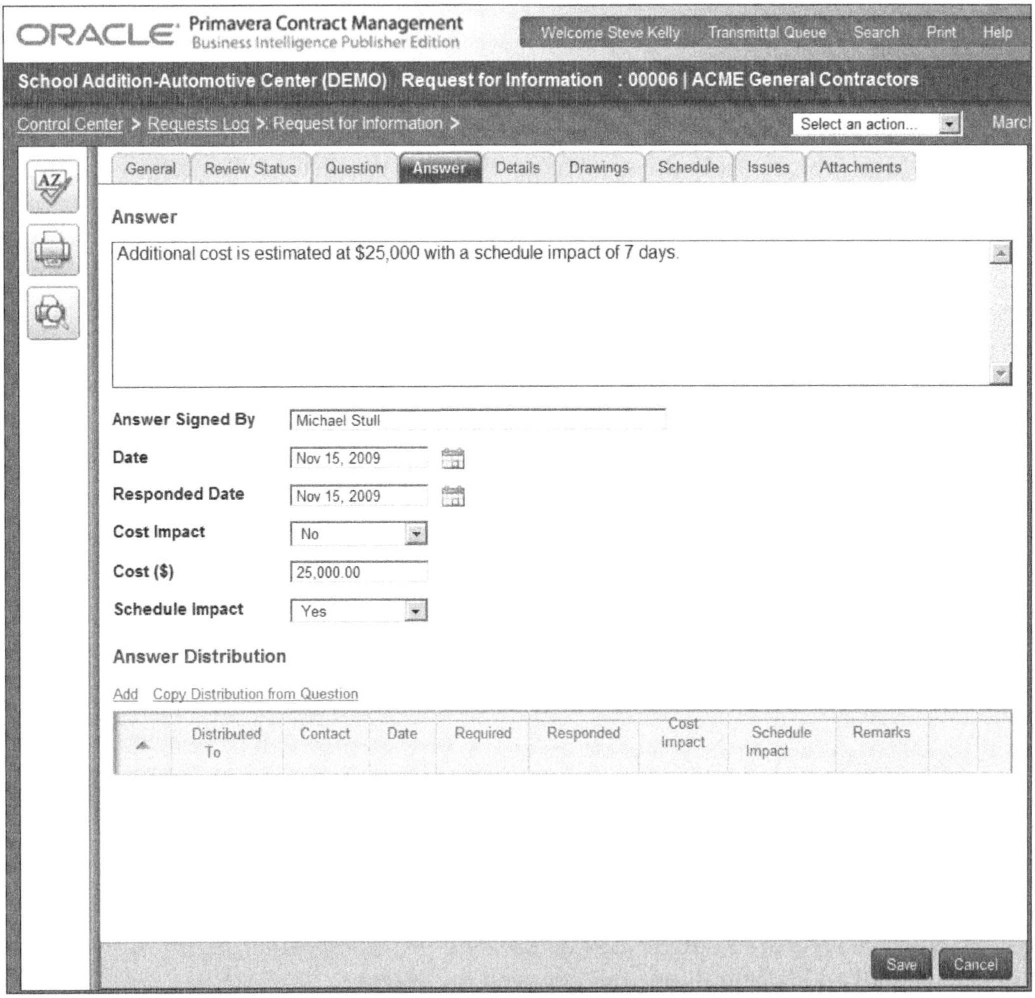

The standard request document is **Request for Information**. PCM allows for multiple Request type documents such as a request for clarification or requests during the pre-construction phase versus the construction phase of the project. Each of these documents can have a unique acronym and therefore a separate register of documents. The uniqueness of the Request module is that it has a tab for questions and a separate tab for answers and these tabs can be assigned their own level of security. It also allows for assignment of multiple drawings from the drawing module to be associated with each document.

This module does not affect the Cost Worksheet, which is discussed in *Chapter 8, Follow the Money*. This is a module where a workflow can be established for approval of the document.

Notices

The Notices module is a fairly generic module. PCM allows for multiple Notice type documents such as an Architectural Supplemental Instruction (ASI) and an Addendum.. This module does not affect the Cost Worksheet. The following screenshot shows the **General** tab of the Notices module in PCM:

It only has a tab for remarks or notes but has a field for date required to be responded. This allows users to review documents that need to be handled before a certain date. The required date is the key to being proactive rather than reactive, or not active at all and letting things fall between the cracks.

Noncompliance Notice

This module is a mixture of the previous modules. It has a tab for recording the problem as well as a tab for recording the solution. It does not have security associated with these tabs as with the Requests. This module does not affect the Cost Worksheet. The following screenshot shows the **Description** tab of the Noncompliance module:

The following screenshot shows the **Corrective Action** tab of the same Notice:

This module allows for the action to the problem to be recorded on the same record. It also has fields for required dates and date that the solution was found. These two simple dates can provide key metrics to understanding response times.

Proposals

This module is designed to work with the Cost Worksheet. This is for any document type that is related to a change prior to the actual Change Order. Examples would be a Change Order Request (COR), a Change Proposal (CP), a Request for Proposal (RFP), any document that records negotiations of a change, and so on.

The following screenshot shows the **General** tab of the Proposal module:

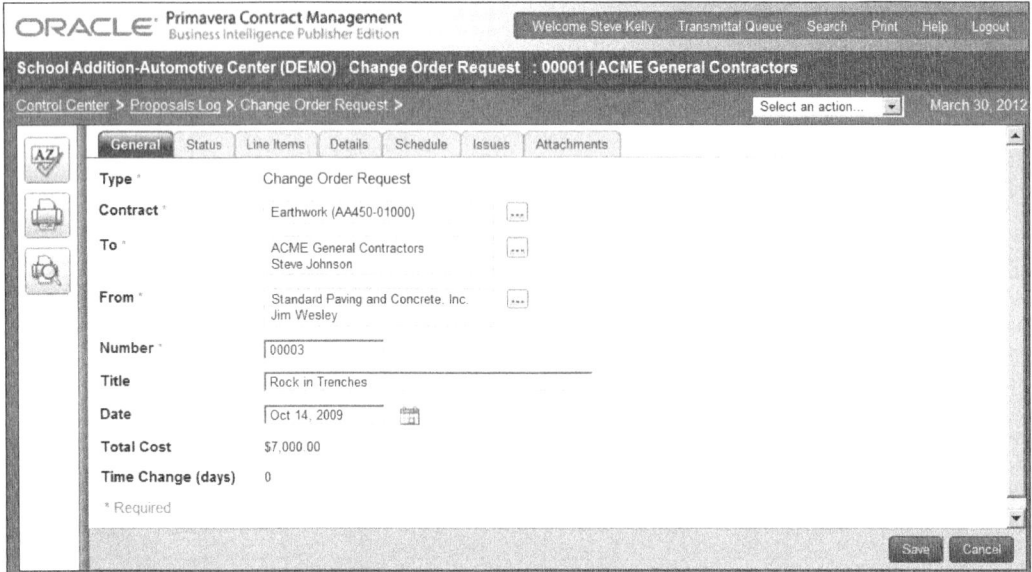

This is the root to managing changes. The proposal is the document that is used in change management to track and record all the communication and negotiations regarding that change up to the final Change Order. Monetary values in the proposal document are placed on the Cost Worksheet. The column on the Cost Worksheet is determined by the workflow design of change management. The proposal document can be either sent from the project or received into the project. The Cost Worksheet and change management will be discussed in more detail in later chapters.

Changes

This module is designed to work with the Cost Worksheet and must also be associated with a Contract/PO in PCM. PCM does not allow a Change document that is not related to a Contract/PO. The following screenshot shows the **General** tab of the Change document:

The Change document allows for collecting of other changes or proposals, or entering the change information directly into this module. This is the final document that can actually change/revise the value of a contract. This document has the ability to be approved and basically locked from any other entry after it is approved. This is another module where a workflow can be established for approval of the document. The following screenshot shows the **Review Status** tab of the Change Order document. The approval workflow is shown at the bottom of the screen.

Summary

There is a definite variety of document types and modules that can be created in PCM. This gives any organization the flexibility it needs to create a system that is best suited to its operations. There is no need to force yourself into an OPC box. The box can be shaped around how you do business. In this chapter we looked at the document types that allow for multiple acronyms, however, there are many other modules (some will be discussed in later chapters) that are designed for different types of information.

In the next chapter we will be looking at the almighty spreadsheet; and while it is the biggest competitor of PCM, it has its drawbacks.

4
The Almighty Spreadsheet

Without a doubt, the spreadsheet is the biggest competitor to PCM or any other contract management application. The great thing about a spreadsheets is "you can do anything you want with it." The worst thing about a spreadsheets is "you can do anything you want with them." While the spreadsheet is an incredible tool to crunch numbers and display data, it is the most overused tool on the planet.

The spreadsheet program started out as rows, columns, creating cells, with the ability to place formulas in cells to perform mathematical calculations. Today, that is about 10 percent or less of what the spreadsheet program can do.

Overusage of the spreadsheet

When you perform a Google search on "how to use a spreadsheet" you will get about 78 million responses, as shown in the following search:

The reasons why people use a spreadsheet vary but we can slim the list down to the following:

- It's easy to use
- It performs simple and complex math easily and quickly
- It has many tools to make it look presentable
- I can make it look exactly the way I want

The spreadsheet program has turned into a data manipulation and presentation tool.

Spreadsheets have a variety of uses; we have all seen them. It is the "one tool does it all" program on every computer in the world. It seems to be the tool of choice even when other tools are better suited or designed for a specific task.

Spreadsheets have been used for the following:

- Word processing
- Flowcharts
- Database storage
- Presentations
- Games

And anything else you can think of.

As discussed in the previous chapter there are many layers of communication. Spreadsheets have the ability to capture layer one, the metadata or the data elements. To take that metadata and place it onto a consistent presentation layer can also be done, but many times the presentation requires information from multiple spreadsheets. We have all seen it: someone is trying to show you his latest spreadsheet creation and errors show up about linked documents not available and so on. The birth of a proper usable spreadsheet is painful and it can be embarrassing when trying to show it off.

A spreadsheet has the capability of taking a long list of rows and sorting and filtering that list pretty easily. It also has the capability of conditional formatting, such as making a cell red if the number is negative, and so on. Without this ability, the spreadsheet might not be so popular for managing project communication. Oh, and let's not forget pivot tables; how can we possibly survive without pivot tables? Regardless of all its cool bells and whistles, the spreadsheet should not be used to manage project control information. Following are just a few obvious reasons.

Accountability

The biggest issue with spreadsheets is the lack of accountability. As stated previously, one of the reasons that spreadsheets are so popular is "I can make it look exactly the way I want." As a manager, that phrase would scare the daylights out of me. Managers should not want a report where the creator has manipulated the data to say whatever he wants it to say. The argument is always brought up that you can lock down cells so this won't happen. Well, if you can lock down cells, you can also unlock those cells. You can save it as a new file and then have full access to the file. The controller of the spreadsheet is the king of that spreadsheet and can manipulate anything he wants. Why force the spreadsheet to do things that other tools are much better suited? Think about all the modules in PCM and then create a spreadsheet for each one with all the locks and programming you would need and then try to link all these spreadsheets together; you see the picture. A spreadsheet is designed for two dimensions; database applications are three dimensional and interlinking within themselves. This should be reason enough to not allow spreadsheets to manage the millions of dollars of project information. Decisions are being made based on the spreadsheet creators making the numbers look exactly the way they want.

My spreadsheet

Creators of spreadsheets are very protective of their creation. It is almost as if it is their child and you have no right to get access to their children whenever you like. It is like the spreadsheet creator is building his own little fiefdom. Some spreadsheet creators are very possessive and do not allow other users access to their creations without specific permissions or else they create a PDF of the spreadsheet for distribution. Do you see the problem with this? If they send you a PDF then you have no idea where the numbers are coming from. You have no idea of any formulae in the background. You just see the data as they want you to see it. Do you think it will ever show the creator in a bad light?

Many spreadsheet creators are programmer-wannabes. Putting a calculation into a spreadsheet cell is paramount to programming in their minds. They feel like they have created their own programs that perform some sort of function automatically. Look out when the spreadsheet creators figure out how to use conditional formatting or even how to write macros. Then they figure out how to place buttons on the spreadsheets to run these super wizbang macros. Quick sort and filtering comes easily so when you watch them at their creations they remind you of a mad scientist mixing together all kinds of chemicals to create some super magic formula for curing the common cold.

Spreadsheet = silo

Spreadsheets are very much a tool used in a siloed approach to management. Each spreadsheet user is his own silo and the spreadsheet is just another tool within that silo. The only way to get information from one silo to the next is for the requestor to ask for the information and the spreadsheet creator to take a snapshot of the spreadsheet (typically PDF), and give it to him. This information is good for a very short time frame if he gets it in a timely matter. As soon as the creator creates that PDF or snapshot of the spreadsheet, there are two documents with the same information. As soon as the creator continues to manipulate the information on the spreadsheet, the PDF is outdated and potentially quite wrong; two copies of the truth, which really is not the truth.

Another scenario is when the creator decides to e-mail his creation to multiple parties for review. The filename might look like the following:

```
my_perfect_creation_for_review.xxx
```

He sends it to five people for review and they all send it back with different names to not confuse anyone or overwrite the original spreadsheet. The reviewed spreadsheets might come back as follows:

```
Bills_response_03_05_12_to_spreadsheet.xxx
my_perfect_creation_SK_03062012.xxx
my_perfect_creation_for_review_harv_3612.xxx
reviewed_ts_comments.xxx
my_perfect_creation_for_review.xxx
```

All of them are spreadsheet files e-mailed back to the creator with various comments (using the fancy comment tool). Now the creator needs to review the comments by opening them side by side with his copy. I think you see the issue here. There are way too many copies, way too many possibilities for errors. It's just a complete mess.

Summary

The spreadsheet is a very powerful tool. It has capabilities beyond what most users understand. It can hold an extremely large amount of data. It has its place in the world of the computerized office, just not in managing critical project information where multiple users and multiple projects are involved. It is a great supporting tool, just not "the" tool for storing and managing any of the project information.

In the next chapter, we will be looking at the answer to not using spreadsheets to manage all this information and the money of your project.

5

There Is a Better Way

So if the spreadsheet is not the answer for mission critical data and processes, then what should be used? Since this is a book about Oracle Primavera Contract Management then obviously that is the alternative we will be discussing throughout the rest of the book. There are also other applications available on the market that perform many of the functions of PCM. Management needs to be able to trust the data to make informed and timely decisions on projects. Use the tools that are designed to provide this information.

What to use

There are many factors to review when deciding on a project management and tracking tool. Every tool on the market has its strengths and weaknesses. Most of them were designed with a specific vertical market in mind and then it was decided to open it up to other markets. PCM was the same way. It was designed with the construction market in mind; however, it has been used in many other vertical markets. Some products are very configurable to the needs of the customer while others are very rigid. Some allow the application to be self-hosted while others are hosted off-site. Some integrate with other applications well while others are rigid with how they share data. Companies need to understand what they need and what is available to make an informed decision.

Following are some factors to consider when deciding on a project management and control tool:

- Accessibility
- Security
- Integration
- Capabilities
- Configuration and customization
- Output

Accessibility

With cloud computing and SaaS (software as a service) readily available to users today, the concept of accessibility should not be a problem. The problem is the difference between self-hosted or outsourced hosting of your application and the requirement that it must be hosted with the application designer. The key to making this decision is the availability of the data, that is, your data. Applications that are hosted on the developer's site and managed by them seem like a nice and clean way to keep and provide project management and communication of project related information until the company goes out of business or is bought by another company. What happens to your data and perhaps even your application? A real world example is Constructware. This was an online (hosted) project management tool that was gaining followers because it was easy to use and you needed no infrastructure or any IT requirements to make it operate. Many owners started requiring that their contractors use this system to communicate on their project. Constructware was sold to Autodesk in 2005 and now doesn't seem to be as big a player in this space. What happened to all those customers that managed their projects on this system? This company looked like it was going places and wasn't even considered a risk, but things happen and it is now a different player with different rules. If you use a hosted system that is still in business, the problem is the data. There is a potential that the hosted system is using a proprietary database system on the back-end and if you want your data, they might offer it, but you might just get a dump of information that is totally unreadable by any other application or database. If your application is self-hosted either on your equipment or on hosted equipment, the data is yours and available to you at any time. You own the data. The last point related to this topic is along the lines of collaboration. This is a subject that really requires its own chapter. In summary, when a customer or owner requires its contractors to use their collaborative system to enter all project related information, the customer thinks he is saving money and providing this "we can all get along and play in the same sandbox" mentality. In reality the customer is paying more on the project as the contractors will oblige and enter the required information in the collaborative system but they will also enter most of the information in their own internal system. Having everyone in the same sandbox is great until someone takes the other person's toy away. When there is litigation, the question then becomes "Who owns the data?" "Who gets to use that data in their defense?"

Security

There is a potential that many users will be accessing the system from all aspects of the project or organization. Users need to be able to perform their jobs, but that is all we want them to do. There needs to be security on various levels. PCM is not the strongest player from the security perspective. It provides many levels of security and is adequate but it has a few holes regarding what users are allowed to see. For example, there is security around "contracts" but not specific to the contract type like Budget or Commitment. If you have access to contracts you have access to all the different types of contracts. Also, there is no field level security in most modules; if users have access to a module, they have access to all fields within that module. One more example is the security setting that allows only documents sent to or from the company of the user to appear in logs. This is a great feature but it is only available for the whole project and is not module specific. There are other applications that have a very robust security model. The problem with security is that no matter what the application allows with regard to security settings, the users would want more. Some of the requirements are access to projects, modules, specific documents, specific fields, process definitions, approvals and at what levels; the list goes on. Review the security model of any application of this magnitude to verify it has the capabilities required by your organization.

Integration

Integration has been a buzzword amongst applications for a long time. Does the application allow data to flow in and out, to or from other applications? Does the system allow for sharing of information to eliminate double entry and to be used to verify information? A project management and control tool has the need to integrate with many other tools in your organization. Following are a few examples of other systems with which you may want to integrate:

- Accounting or ERP
- Scheduling application
- Document control system
- E-mail
- CAD/CAM
- BIM
- Websites
- Photo management
- Document viewers and markup

The list is almost endless. Any tool you use in your organization can either use information from another tool or offer information to other systems.

There are some solutions that provide some of the other tools as well, so integration should be easy and complete with those tools. An example of that is the Timberline suite of accounting and estimating tools, which now has a project controls module that seamlessly operates as one application. Having a full suite of tools under one roof is not necessarily the best solution. Most companies have a core product that has made them successful and then they try to add the other tools. Another example is the Oracle Primavera suite of tools. This integration is discussed in *Chapter 15, P6 and PCM*. A serious look should be taken when selecting tools for your organization. Take a serious look at what the industry considers as the "best of breed" solutions.

Some applications are written with hooks into PCM. They know how to talk to PCM and therefore are more robust in the integration. However, these tools are often very rigid in how they handle the data and place it in specific places that may not be where you want to see it, while others are designed for ease of use as with several third party integration tools including an intuitive user interface.

Capabilities

Not all software is the same. Does the tool perform all the functions required by your organization? Many of the project control tools available now do not have all the abilities that you want or need. Some are very good at jobsite related information but are poor at the cost control aspects. Some are exactly the opposite. PCM has 33 different modules that are designed to cover all aspects of project communication and cost control. It even has some generic modules such as **Notepads** that can contain information that may not specifically fit in other modules. Be sure that all project communication and cost controls can be managed using the processes of your organization in one tool. It does not make sense to have some of your project communication in one tool and other information in other applications. If all the information is in one tool then searching for information becomes easier and more efficient.

Configuration and customization

These aspects are completely different and yet they are together in this section because they are many times used interchangeably. There is a big difference between configuration and customization.

Configuration is the ability to change various aspects of the application using the user interface. These changes may be required by an administrator but the user interface is used to make these changes.

Customization is the ability to change various aspects or add functionality to the application through custom written programming. Typically this is done to the backend of the application and requires a programmer to write the scripts or code for the new functionality. Many times there is an application programming interface (API) or Web Services available that allow a programmer to write new screens for entering data or to properly extract data from the application, but this is still customization.

Both of these aspects have their advantages and the ability to perform both can be advantageous to your organization. There is no such thing as *perfect* software. There is always some aspect of the application that needs to be adjusted or changed to meet the needs of the organization. Configuration typically does not affect any aspect of the application. This process is merely changing the terminology or creating workflows, and so on, to match your organization and are intended to be changed by the application. PCM has several avenues to allow the organization to configure the application to mirror their processes. Some of these include custom fields, customized text, configurable project tree, and configurable dictionaries.

Customization typically utilizes an API or Web Services of some sort to properly connect to the application and utilize the proper business rules of the application but requires custom programming to achieve the desired result. Many times customization can go too far and not use the proper tools (APIs) to properly talk to the application, such as inserting records into the database with an ODBC connection; this bypasses any application business rules and opens up the application to inconsistencies and data integrity problems. It may also affect any upgrades to the application distributed by the software vendor such as Oracle. Some applications will void the warranty if a customization is written outside of the API or Web Services.

Output

Entering data into a system is all fine and good but if you cannot get the information out of the system in an easy-to-read and understandable format, it's time to look for another system. The output is critical to allowing management and the users to review and analyze the information entered. You need to question the need to enter certain data elements if they are not reviewed or reported on at some time. There are several forms of output from PCM as follows:

- Forms
- Reports
- Letters
- Dunning Letters

Let's review what each of these types of output include and how they are used with relation to PCM.

Forms

The forms (or templates) are similar to a form fill. PCM uses the metadata entered into the various fields of a module to produce a form for printing or e-mailing for distribution to one or multiple recipients. These templates provide a consistency of output across the projects for your organization. All projects can use the same set of templates, or a new set of templates can be created for a specific project if required. An example of this is the Request for Information form. The metadata is entered into the system using the RFI module. When the user is ready to send out the information to an outside party he or she prints a form and distributes it. The following screenshot shows the screen where RFIs are entered:

The following screenshot is the corresponding form (template) that can be produced from PCM. The templates can be customized using the BI Publisher report writer.

```
🖨 💾 🖋 ▾   🌐   ⬆ ⬇   1 / 1   ⊝ ⊕  84.8% ▾   ⬛ ⬚   Find                    ▾
```

Mechanical Contractors	REQUEST FOR INFORMATION
1400 Darby Road	No. 00004

1400 Darby Road   **Phone:** 610-555-3333
Havertown, PA 19000   **Fax:** 610-555-3330

TITLE: Pipe Cleanout   **DATE:** 08/31/2009
PROJECT: School Addition-Automotive Center   **JOB:** JBAA450
TO: Attn: Steve Johnson
           ACME General Contractors
           1001 South Street   **STARTED:**
           Philadelphia, PA 19100   **COMPLETED:**
           Phone: 215-555-2011   Fax: 215-555-6889   **REQUIRED:**   09/09/2009

QUESTION:

The Underground Utilities Change includes rerouting existing piping around the new building foundation. There is no pipe cleanout on the existing piping - based on the new location of the piping, it would make sense to install one.

ANSWER:

Yes, please provide pricing for new pipe cleanout.

Reports

In a simple way a report is just a listing of selected metadata of multiple records. There are several parameters that can be defined in the report to determine what records to display and how they are displayed. Reporting is very important to the success of your organization as there is potential for tens of thousands of records of information to be managed; how do you know what information you need to concentrate your time on? The following parameters can be used to help restrict and display the data:

- **Filtering**: It's used to restrict the records by a filter of metadata
- **Sorting**: It's used to organize the filtered list by one or more metadata elements
- **Grouping**: It's used to highlight the sorted data into intelligent bands

For example, there can be a report listing all RFI data elements with no filter applied. This is basically a data dump of the RFI module. It would be massive as there are many available data elements in the RFI module master record and there could be a hundred or more records in your project. If you were looking for the RFIs that are overdue to be answered, it would be an extremely tedious task to find those records amongst all that information. We are in the computer age. We can use the power of filtering and sorting to present to us an output that takes little time to understand and take action.

If you applied a filter on the same report that would exclude all RFIs that have been closed as well as the RFIs that already have a date entered in the Required Answer field, and only selected the key metadata such as RFI number, date, title, and so on and sorted it in reverse order by the date it was required to be answered, the searching for the specific RFIs that you need to concentrate your time on is no longer necessary; the computer has searched for you. There is great power in reporting as long as all users are using the same reports. Reports should be designed and implemented in the system and not available to be changed or adjusted without going through proper change management procedures. Allowing for exporting to a spreadsheet to give the user more flexibility in reporting is not acceptable (see *Chapter 4*, *The Almighty Spreadsheet*). This just gives the user the power to manipulate the data and you are no longer looking at controlled data. The following screenshot is an example of an RFI report:

Another type of reporting is the **Exception** report. These reports are designed to highlight records that have missing or improper information. As long as there are humans entering data there will be an element of error. Exception reporting can be designed to catch this information as well as the users that do not completely enter all the information required. For example, an exception report can be designed to show all the RFIs where the required answer date field is left blank. If that field is required to be filled in by company policy, a report showing me all the RFIs where this is not being done would be helpful. If this data is not being populated, my earlier report of finding all the RFIs where the answer is overdue will not work properly.

Reporting can be done across multiple modules and multiple projects as required. There is a vast amount of intelligence that can be placed in reporting to provide the users and management information they need to help them understand where to spend their valuable time.

Letters

The Letters module has to be placed in this list as it is another area where information can be printed and distributed. The Letters module is unique in that it allows users to free form type information into the body of the letter with limited tracking of metadata. There are a few fields of metadata that are stored in the master record of PCM before the letter is actually produced but there is so much more that is said in the body of the letter that cannot be reported in a columnar format. This module can be designed with consistency of output in mind as it uses BI Publisher to create the letter templates in which the balance of the letter can be entered. For example, the template can include all the header and footer information by placing data elements from the master record onto the page. This leaves only the body of the letter to be typed by the user.

Dunning Letters

This is a special type of letter where the complete layout and content of the letter is predefined. Then the letter is sent out on a regular basis to individuals that meet a criteria. For instance, you can create dunning letters to inform all companies that have insurance expiring in two weeks. The system looks at the expiration date of all insurance policies entered in PCM and determines if they warrant a letter based on that date. The body of the dunning letter is predefined with various company-specific elements inserted if needed.

PCM v14 uses Oracle BI Publisher as its report writing engine. This tool is extremely powerful and the PCM community should be seeing more of this power unleashed with future releases.

There are options

When looking for the perfect project controls application for your business, understand that this perfect tool does not exist. The only way for the perfect tool that encompasses all aspects of your specific processes and procedures to exist is to write the application in-house. The problem with this approach is you are not in the software development business. The cost of developing, maintaining, updating, and supporting a tool as big as project controls requires many resources and lots of money. There are many "off the shelf" tools available that will provide a high percentage of the features you need to properly manage your business. PCM is just one of them; however, it is the tool that is most widely used around the country and internationally and is the tool by which others are measured.

Since the perfect tool does not exist, you need to analyze all the features that you must have and then prepare a list of nice-to-haves. Analyze each application and review its functionality. Be sure and have the organization that represents the tool to talk to you about their tool and all the bells and whistles it has to offer. Then be sure and have an independent consultant tell you the real story about the tools and their advantages and disadvantages. Sometimes it is advantageous to have an independent consult in the interviews with the vendors to ask certain questions. Either way, ask a lot of questions. Get other opinions. Ask more questions. Get more opinions.

Summary

Understand that finding, configuring, implementing, testing, and training an application of this magnitude is not a small project. Be prepared for many meetings with lengthy discussions to understand exactly what the business needs. It is best to get outside help in making these decisions as outsiders typically see things that insiders do not. They typically don't care about the people whose answer is, "that is always the way we have done it." An outsider has no inside bias and many times can help to get past the corporate politics and provide meaningful analysis of your organization and its needs.

The next chapter will start with the thirty-thousand foot view of the concepts of using PCM specifically the money and the hierarchy, which is key to managing projects.

6

The Big Picture

It's time to get down to the details of PCM. To understand the details, we must understand the big picture of what it is designed to do. You can look at PCM from many different angles or roles. It is designed such that multiple levels of the organization have some sort of access into the system to input, analyze, query, or review information. Like any other system, the quality and reliability of the analysis is only as good as the quality of the data entered. Organizations that embrace PCM at all levels are the organizations that gain the most from the system. PCM is merely a tool to be used. It does not perform functions on its own; it relies on quality input to provide quality information for precise, timely project decisions.

Thirty-thousand foot view

As we look down upon PCM from a high level, there are many aspects that need to be understood. There is nothing magical about PCM; it is not performing any function that cannot be done manually or with a strictly paper system. It is simply a digital filing cabinet; no more, no less. Back in time, before the advent of the computer, projects were run with paper, the mail system, and a filing cabinet (two or three or many more file cabinets). These were the information, delivery system, and storage, respectively. Without a computer we still dealt with lots of information. We had to have a means of distributing it and the US Postal Service was the only game in town, and we had to have a way to store this information. The computer age has allowed us to use the computer for all of these requirements. The needs are the same, but the tools are different.

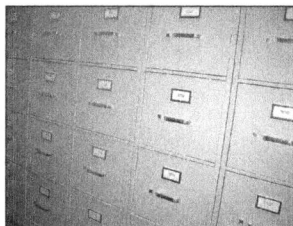

Back when our cavemen friends were building things, they needed to dig a foundation for a building. The only tool they had was a rock tied to a stick. Today, we still have the need to dig a foundation but the tools are much different. Why did we change from the stick and rock? One word: efficiency. The digging tools today are much faster and more accurate, therefore, much more efficient. Can we still dig a hole with a stick and a rock? Of course we can, but why would you do that when there are better, more efficient tools around? The same is true for project controls. Can we still manage a project with paper, the US Postal Service, and filing cabinets? Of course, but there are significantly more efficient tools on the market that provide faster and more accurate information for making informed decisions. PCM is simply a glorified file cabinet that can provide information on a document, deliver it electronically and store it for retrieval later. And when you retrieve it in an electronic format, it is still the same information – not the faded thermal fax paper of years gone by.

Looking down upon PCM from thirty thousand feet, we see a multi-project, multi-user, secure, browser-based, and single location for all information on a project. In theory, any aspect of communication and project costs should be available from PCM. PCM is designed to work best as a post contract award system; therefore it fits in the execution phase of the project. Once the project has been declared and a budget has been approved the project can be created. Even though PCM has a procurement module, it is not very robust and cannot compete with the larger ERP systems' procurement modules. If your organization is not using one of the large ERP systems, the Procurement module within PCM should work fine for analyzing and awarding commitment contracts; however, PCM truly shines after the contract has been awarded.

The money

The monetary aspect of the project and contracts is the core of PCM. All other modules are built around this core. This is the main differentiator between PCM and many of the other systems on the market. PCM is built on the contractual relationship. The contractual relationship is the center of the universe as far as PCM is concerned. The center of the monetary aspect of PCM is the **Cost Worksheet** module. All monetary entries into PCM will be placed someplace on the Cost Worksheet (More on these details in *Chapter 8, Follow the Money*). There are many documents in PCM that deal with money, such as the following:

- Contracts – Budget
- Contracts – Committed
- Contracts – Custom
- Purchase Orders

- Change Orders to all the above contract types and Purchase Orders
- Proposals related to all the above contract types and Purchase Orders
- Payment Requisitions
- Invoices
- Trends

Other modules that deal with money but are not necessarily document records are as follows:

- Cost Worksheet
- Change Management
- Procurement

Any entry of money in these documents/modules will automatically populate the Cost Worksheet. The Cost Worksheet is the core of all monetary transactions within PCM.

A matter of perspective

To properly operate PCM you need to understand from what perspective you are looking at the project. PCM can be used from all perspectives, but only one perspective can be used when setting up a group of projects. The perspective you choose depends on where your company resides in the project hierarchy. A simple hierarchy is listed in the following figure. The Owner has a relationship with a Contractor, an Engineer, and a Project Management firm. The Contractor has a relationship with a Subcontractor and Supplier. And the Subcontractor has a relationship with its Supplier.

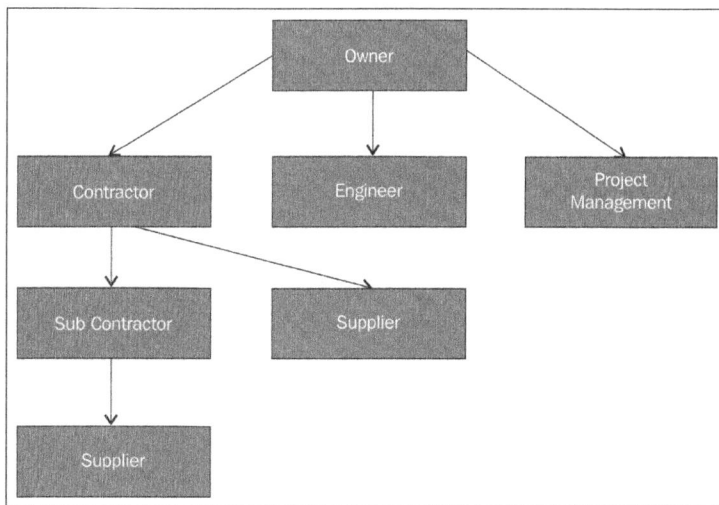

Typically your organization looks at all your projects from the same perspective. For example, let's revisit our cavemen. The project hierarchy for the self-propelled chair is as follows:

- Owner – Kristin
- Builder – Joe
- Supplier – David

Each of them can use PCM but they are looking at the project from different perspectives.

- The Owner is managing a budget amount of money that he has set aside for the building of this chair, let's say 50,000 stones. He is also managing a contract he has in place with the Builder, for 40,000 stones. In this example, he is anticipating a 10,000 stone potential overrun and has money available to him if the cost of the chair goes over the contract value.

- The Builder is managing a contract he has in place with the Owner, for 40,000 stones. This is the exact same contract as the one described above for the Owner, but he is looking at it from a different perspective. This is 40,000 stones he will receive if he builds the chair according to the contract. For the Owner, it is 40,000 stones he will spend to get this new chair. Same contract, but different perspective. The Builder is also managing contracts with Suppliers for parts to the chair.

- The Supplier is managing a contract with the Builder to supply parts for the chair. Again, the same contract but from two different perspectives.

You must select a perspective to use PCM for your projects. You cannot view a project in PCM from all perspectives. PCM only allows for one perspective to be used for each Group (database) of projects as an example. The contract between the Owner and the Builder is a commitment contract from the Owner's perspective but that same contract is a budget contract from the Builder's perspective, or at the least an internal reckoning of costs and profits.

It's not only the money aspect that is different. By selecting your perspective, PCM will determine whom documents will be written to and whom they will be from. If an RFI is written on the project, the exact same document will seem different depending on your perspective. If the RFI is a question regarding what type of wood the Owner wants to use for the chair, then from the Owner's perspective it is a document received into his project and from the Builder's perspective it is a document sent from his project.

To select the perspective, use the **Companies** tab in the **Project Settings** or when you are starting a project. The field labeled **Your Company** is the perspective from which PCM views the project. The following screenshot shows the screen where the various roles for a project are determined and therefore the perspective to which the project is assigned. Assigning your company to the **Your Company** field on this screen seems obvious, but it determines the perspective to which PCM will be viewing the project.

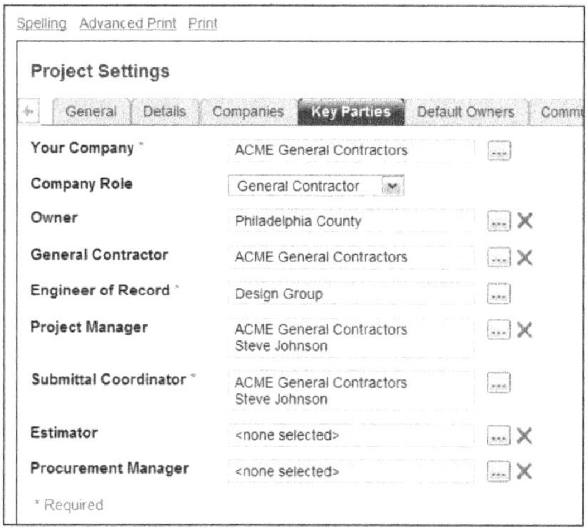

Once the perspective is selected, all the modules in the system fall into place. PCM will assign the default **To** and **From** companies for most of the modules automatically. These defaults can be changed in the **Default Field Values** window, as shown in the following screenshot:

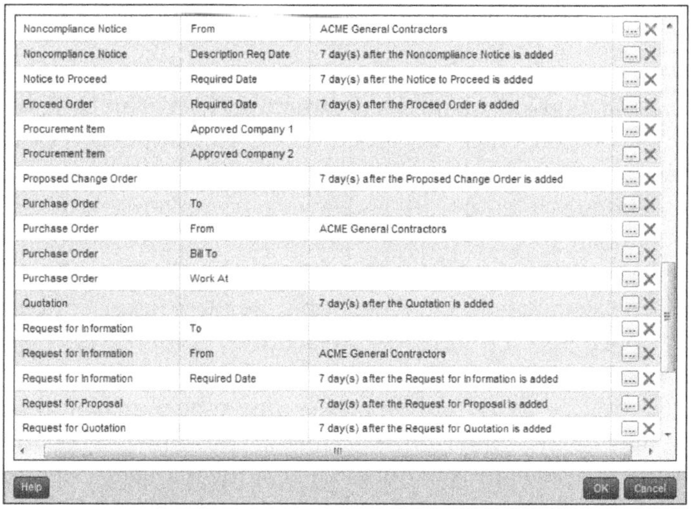

Understanding the hierarchy

There are two basic types of hierarchies we need to consider when using PCM. There is the project hierarchy and the monetary hierarchy. Each of these structures allows for the rolling up of information to the various levels within the hierarchy. Security is not based on either of these hierarchical structures as it is assigned by the user at the project level only.

Project hierarchy

The project hierarchy is developed using the project tree on the opening screen of PCM. PCM can hold up to nine different tree configurations as required by the organization. It is a simple way to organize your projects into a hierarchical structure. The following screenshot is an example of a project hierarchical structure:

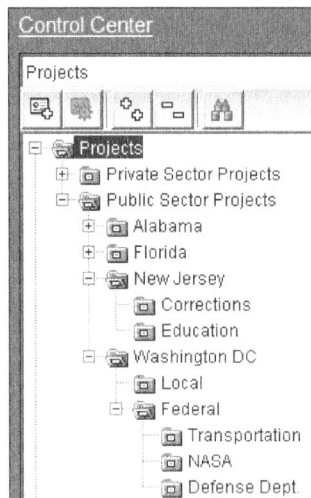

All projects are part of a project hierarchical structure. There can be very simple structures and very complex ones. Large, multinational companies can have a complex project hierarchical structure. Each project (which the *Project Management Body of Knowledge Guide* defines as a temporary endeavor undertaken to create a unique product, service, or result) is placed somewhere within this hierarchy. That does not mean that it can't move within the hierarchy. There may also be multiple hierarchical structures within an organization. PCM can replicate these simple or complex hierarchies for the purposes of rolling up information for review and reporting. PCM even allows for a project to be included in multiple locations of the hierarchy. For example, if you have a tree configuration broken down by manager, there could be a case where there may be two managers working on the same project. In this case you would want to place the same project under each of the managers in the tree.

Defining the "project" in PCM can be difficult at times. Many factors are considered when making this decision:

- Are there multiple contracts to be released within the same project?
- Are there different funding sources to be considered?
- How will the costs be rolled up?
- How will the documents be managed?
- How will the contracts and Purchase Orders be managed?

There are always exceptions to these rules when deciding upon where to place the project in PCM. There is another option of creating a completely different Group (set of projects) that may have a drastically different definition. The project in PCM is the defining location between this hierarchy and the available modules in PCM. Every "project" has its own set of modules.

The cost hierarchy

The cost hierarchy can be called the Cost Breakdown Structure (CBS) or Cost Accounts in some organizations. This is how the money is broken down within a project. Many companies have a standard CBS that they use on all projects. This is extremely beneficial for roll-up analysis and reporting. The Cost Code has a maximum of 30 characters including any separation characters such as dots or dashes. You can create as many segments as you need within that thirty-character limit. This structure often mimics your accounting cost breakdowns, especially if you plan on integrating your accounting system with PCM.

The cost breakdown is a database level hierarchy. This means that the cost breakdown levels are created at the database level and then used by all projects. However, there are ways to circumvent this restriction by using a segment of the Cost Code for project specific information. To create the cost breakdown you use the **Cost Code Definitions** option from the project tree. The following screenshot shows the **Cost Code Definitions** window:

Cost Code Definitions   help

Add

	Definition Name	Description	Start	Length	
	Phase	Phase	1	2	delete
	Facility	Facility	4	3	delete
	Discipline	Discipline	8	2	delete
	SubDiscipline	Sub-Discipline	11	3	delete
	Category	Category	15	1	delete

In this window you define what characters relate to which subsection of the Cost Code. Each of the segments of the Cost Code can then be populated with a dictionary of possible codes for that segment. For example, consider the following Cost Code:

`Cost Code 01-401-26-001-S`

Using the structure in the previous screenshot, this Cost Code can be interpreted as shown in the following table:

Cost Code Example	
Segment	**Example**
Phase	01
Facility	401
Discipline	26
Sub-Discipline	001
Category	S

Each of the segments listed in the table can have a dictionary of possible codes and the titles of those codes. For instance, there may be five facilities for a project. The dictionary would carry the code used for each of the facilities and the corresponding title or description of those facilities. This will be discussed in more detail in *Chapter 8, Follow the Money*.

The overall hierarchical structure for your organization includes both of these individual hierarchies. The following diagram shows an example of the many hierarchical levels using the example structures shown previously in this chapter:

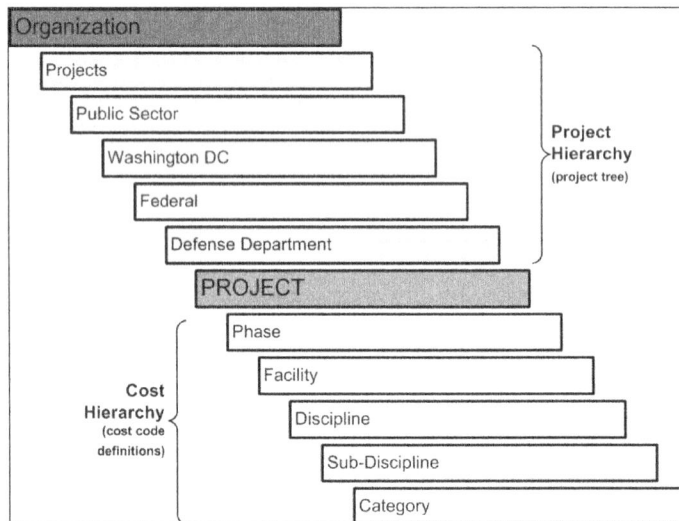

Summary

Understanding your perspective on a project determines how PCM sees the money and the documents on that project. Understanding the hierarchical structure of your organization allows you to properly place the project in PCM with the ability to break costs down to a very granular level of detail.

In the next chapter, we will look into the concept of system versus silo and how PCM can break down the silos in your organization.

7
System versus Silo

The word silo is overused today but it really does fit when talking about managing projects. Even though the word silo has negative connotations in today's world, many projects still function with a siloed approach to management. This is reinforced by the widespread use of the spreadsheet discussed in Chapter 4, The Almighty Spreadsheet. If the contract administrator, the submittal coordinator, the cost engineer, and the project manager all run spreadsheets to manage their information, they are running in their own little silos. At the risk of being stoned for this cliché, break down the silos and use an integrated system.

Typical silo approach

The concept of a silo is a walled container where all the information for that particular process is nicely stored together, which is great if you are working in the silo, but making access to that information for other departments difficult. Each process or department has its own container or silo. If one silo needs information from another silo, someone must go to that silo and see if the owner of the information is available or if he is willing to give that information. The siloed approach has been around for a long time with the manager of the silo keeping their fiefdoms, or should we say "silo-doms", to themselves and only releasing information to others if they see fit or when they are ready.

What's wrong with this approach

Prior to the advent of the personal computer, there were mainframe computers that stored important company information. These mainframe computers used terminals to access them. There was no storage on the terminals, just an access point to the mainframe. The applications and the data were all on that mainframe computer. No silo allowed here.

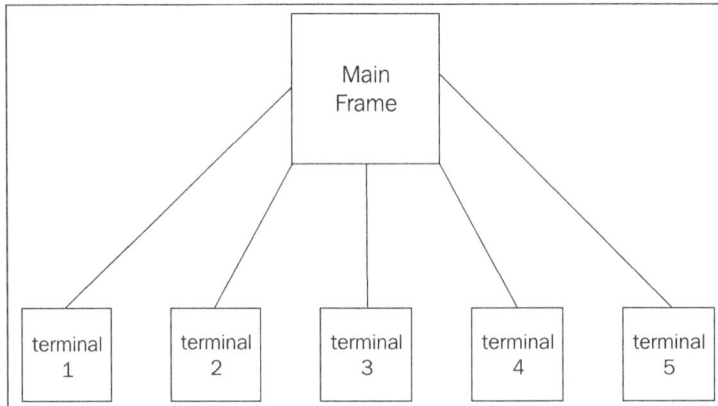

Enter the personal computer. This allows individuals to keep all their information in their own personal storage space and only when someone asks for this information would they be able to provide it. This was a fantastic breakthrough as the computers were on the desktop and no connection to the mainframe was necessary. This automatically bred the silo approach to information. The only way to get information from another user was to ask him for it and perhaps he provided it on a floppy disk.

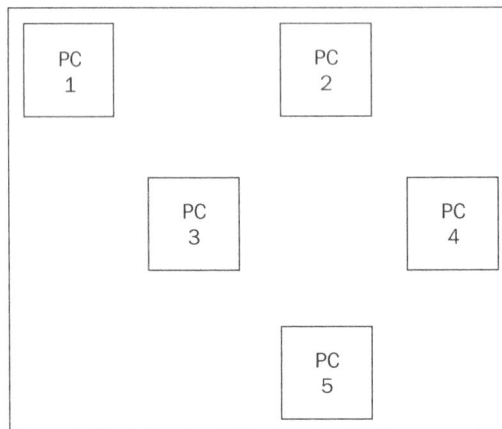

The concept of the office computer network helped break down some of those silo walls but as long as users could still store things on their personal machines, they only placed information on the network that was requested or required. Many times you still had to ask for a file to get information. Users had complete control of the information. They were very protective of their information.

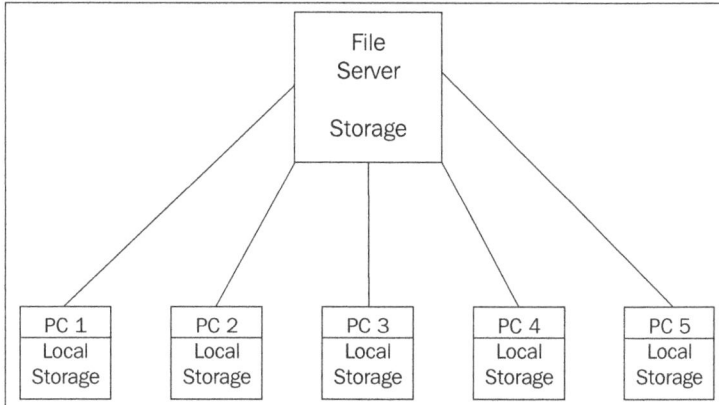

The word accountability was, and still is today, a scary word. Users have the idea that if there is some information that they have provided, they are responsible for it and should be held accountable. What a concept! It seems that the culture of today is to cover yourself so you don't get blamed if something goes wrong. So they hold onto their information very close to the chest and only provide exactly what has been requested and only when it is requested.

The silo approach breeds inefficiency and the concept of my data versus project data. Users like to have control of their information and are reluctant to release it. The time it takes to ask for this information and the subsequent conversation (usually via e-mail) that goes on to obtain it can be quite large. There is a lot of wasted time getting users to release their information. They are afraid it might be scrutinized or there may be an error that can be pinned on them. If they can just keep it in their silo then maybe no one will notice the potential issues. This is false thinking; issues always come to light eventually. With the siloed approach usually it is too late.

There are many excuses as to why the silo approach is good. Many departments and users feel that the information they are holding is sensitive and should not be visible to others in the organization. While this may be true, in most cases it is not. Each department claims that the company can't survive without them and therefore its information is sacred. In actuality every department in the company could claim this perspective, but this type of thinking makes every department feel it is unique to the company and therefore should be treated special.

When a problem comes up on a project or in your organization, the silo thinker either looks at that situation and claims it all as his own and that he will fix it or he completely divorces himself from it. This type of business means that each silo is its own entity with no other influence or support from the other silos.

The system approach

An organization run by a system is open and streamlined. The system is applied across all departments and users. There are still specific departments or roles with proper security associated that perform their tasks, but the information they enter and manage is not restricted from the other departments that need the information. All the information required for a department to properly manage and make decisions is available to them, whether produced in their department or not. A system approach means that all departments within an organization are responsible for the outcome of the project; there are no hidden agendas.

Organizations that use spreadsheets and word documents are typically operating silos. These documents are owned by an individual or department and typically are not available to all parties that could use the information. If the information were placed in a system, the information required would be available and efficient management becomes possible.

It is not easy to change an organization from silos to system. To do this requires a mindset change and it is very hard for the mind to change its ways. Many times it requires removal of those individuals who will not change this mindset. This type of change is not something that can happen overnight. It requires a systematic change of procedures and adoption of new procedures before you move to the next stage of your conversion. This is also a decision that must come from upper management and be driven by that level of management. It can be very difficult for some managers to make waves in their organization. They would prefer to just keep the status quo. The old saying, "If it ain't broke, don't fix it" comes to mind. Many times the problem is that managers don't know it is broken. If you were to sit in a standard shift car after driving an automatic for many years and just drove down the road without ever shifting into second gear, you would think that is normal. With your experience in driving, you got into the car, started it, and drove off; there was nothing else to do. So in your mind driving in first gear everywhere was normal. You didn't get to places very fast, the engine made a heck of a noise when you were on the freeway, and people on the freeway that passed you at a high speed had some special gestures for you as they passed, but it was normal. You knew that the car wasn't like your old car but it did the job and that was okay. You had no idea that the car could be much more efficient if you would learn how to shift into the other gears. It wasn't broken per se, but it had a lot more horsepower that you were not tapping into. It's the same with implementing a system approach. The silo approach works; it gets the job done, but your processes can be much more efficient and you won't have people giving you hand gestures along the way. Obviously PCM is a system where with the proper security, all users and roles on a project have access to the information they need. When changing from a silo to a system using a tool like PCM, the roles need to realize that other roles are dependent on them to enter their data in a timely matter so the work can get done efficiently. A system is only as efficient as the users using it.

Summary

The silo approach to running an organization has been around for many years. It is the preferred method for users as they can then protect their information. They can run their own fiefdoms. Don't take the easy road; take the road that is efficient. The efficient road that works is the system approach where all information related to a project is in one location for the proper users to see and analyze.

In the next chapter we will be switching gears and looking at how to follow the money on your project using the system approach and PCM.

8
Follow the Money

The money is at the core of PCM. All documents in PCM related to money are also related to a specific contractual relationship defined in PCM (trends being a possible exception). And since the contractual relationship is the center of the universe as far as PCM is concerned, it follows that managing the money is at the core of the system. If you understand the information in this chapter you will be far ahead of most users of PCM, and all the other chapters will make more sense.

It starts with the Cost Worksheet

In PCM, the Cost Worksheet is the common element for all the monetary modules. The Cost Worksheet is a spreadsheet-like module with rows and columns. The following screenshot shows a small part of a typical **Cost Worksheet** register:

	Cost Code	Title	Original Budget	Approved Budget Revisions
	01 01100 O	Summary	$240,000.00	$0.00
	01 01300 D	Administration Requirements	$274,264.12	$0.00
	01 01300 O	Adminstration Reqmnts - Schedule	$244,500.00	$0.00
	01 01400 S	Quality Requirements - Testing	$65,000.00	$0.00
	01 01400 W	Quality Requirements - Software	$7,735.68	$0.00

ORACLE Primavera Contract Management
Business Intelligence Publisher Edition

School Addition-Automotive Center (DEMO) Cost Worksheet

Control Center > Cost Worksheet

The columns are set by PCM but the rows are determined by the organization. The rows are the Cost Codes. This is your cost breakdown structure. This is the lowest level of detail with which money will be tracked in PCM. It can also be called Cost Accounts. All money entered into the documents in any of the monetary modules in PCM *will* be allocated to a Cost Code on the Cost Worksheet. Even if you do not specifically allocate to a Cost Code, the system will allocate to a system generated Cost Code called NOT COSTED. The NOT COSTED Cost Code is important so no money slips through the cracks. If you forget to assign money to your Cost Codes on the project it will assign the money to this code. When reviewing the Cost Worksheet, a user can review the NOT COSTED Cost Code and see if any money is associated with this code. If there is money associated with NOT COSTED, he can find that document where he has forgotten to allocate all the money to proper Cost Codes. Users cannot edit any numbers directly on the Cost Worksheet; it is a reflection of information entered on various documents on your project. This provides a high level of accountability in that no money can be entered or changed without a document entered someplace within PCM (like can be done with a spreadsheet)

The Cost Code itself can be up to 30 characters in length and can be divided into segments to align with the cost breakdown structure, as shown in the following screenshot:

The number of Cost Codes and the level of breakdown is typically determined by the accounting or ERP system used by your organization or it can be used as an extension of the ERP system's coding structure. When the Cost Code structure matches, integration between the two systems becomes easier. There are many other factors to consider when thinking about integrating systems but the Cost Code structure is at the core of relating the two systems.

Defining the segments within the Cost Codes is done as part of the initial setup and implementation of PCM. This is done in the **Cost Code Definitions** screen, as shown in the following screenshot:

Cost Code Definitions				help
Add				
▲ Definition Name	Description	Start	Length	
☑ DIVI	CSI Division	1	2	delete
☑ SPEC	Specification Section	4	5	delete
☑ CATG	Cost Category	10	1	delete

To set up, you must tell PCM what character of the Cost Code the segment starts with and how long the segment is (the number of characters). Once this is done you can also populate a dictionary of titles for each segment. A trick used for having different segment titles for different projects is to create an identical segment dictionary but for different projects. For example, if you have a different list of Disciplines for every project, you can create and define a list of Disciplines for each project with the same starting character and length. Then you can use the proper Cost Code definitions in your layouts and reporting for that project. The following screenshot shows how this can be done:

Cost Code Definitions				
Add				
▲ Definition Name	Description	Start	Length	
☑ Phase	Phase	1	2	delete
☑ Facility	Facility			delete
☑ Discipline	Discipline	8	2	delete
☑ PROJA_DISC	Proj A - Discipline	8	2	delete
☑ PROJB_DISC	Proj B - Discipline	8	2	delete
☑ SubDiscipline	SubDiscipline			delete
☑ Category	Category	10	1	delete

Once the Cost Codes have been defined, the Cost Worksheet will need to be populated for your project. There are various ways to accomplish this.

- Create a dummy project with the complete list of company Cost Codes you would ever use on a project. When you want to populate the Cost Code list on a new project, use the Copy Cost Codes function from the project tree.

- Import a list of Cost Codes that have been developed in a spreadsheet (Yes, I used the word "spreadsheet". There are times when a spreadsheet comes in handy – managing a multi-million dollar project is not one of them). PCM has an import function from the Cost Worksheet where you can import a comma-separated values (CSV) file of the Cost Codes and titles.

- Enter the Cost Codes one at a time from the Cost Worksheet. If there are a small number of Cost Codes, this might be the fastest and easiest method.

Understanding the columns of the Cost Worksheet will help you understand how powerful and important the Cost Worksheet really is. The columns of the Cost Worksheet in PCM are set by the system. They are broken down into a few categories, as follows:

- Budget
- Commitment
- Custom
- Actuals
- Procurement
- Variances
- Miscellaneous

Each of the categories has a corresponding color to help differentiate them when looking at the Cost Worksheet.

Within each of these categories are a number of columns. The Budget, Commitment, and Custom categories have the same columns while the other categories have their own set of columns. These three categories work basically the same. They can be defined in basic terms as follows:

- **Budget**: This is the money that your company has available to spend and is going to be received by the project. Examples depend on the perspective of the setup of PCM discussed in *Chapter 6, The Big Picture*. In the example of our cavemen Joe and David, David is the person working for Joe. If David was using PCM, the Budget category would be the amount of the agreed price between Joe and David to make the chair or the amount of money that David was going to be paid by Joe to make the chair.

- **Committed**: This is the money that has been agreed to be spent on the project, not the money that has been spent. So in our example it would be the amount of money that David has agreed to pay his subcontractors to supply him with goods and services to build the chair for him.

- **Custom**: This is a category that is available to be used by the user for another contracting type. It has its own set of columns identical to the Budget and Commitment categories. This can be used for a Funding module where you can track the amount of money funded for the project, which can be much different from the available budget for the project.

> Money distributed to the Trends module can be posted to many of the columns as determined by the user upon adding the Trend. The Trends module will be discussed with relationship to forecasting in Chapter 11, Reading your Crystal Ball. The Trend document is not referenced in the following explanations.

When money is entered in a document, it must be allocated or distributed to one or multiple Cost Codes. As stated before, if you forget or do not allocate the money to a Cost Code, PCM will allocate the money to the NOT COSTED Cost Code. The system knows what column to place the money in but the user must tell PCM the proper row (Cost Code). If the Status Type of a document is set to Closed or Rejected, the money is removed from the Cost Worksheet but the document is still available to be reviewed. This way only documents that are in progress or approved will be placed on the Cost Worksheet. Let's look at each of the columns individually and explain how money is posted.

The only documents that affect the Cost Worksheet are as follows:

- Contracts (three types)
- Change Orders
- Proposals
- Payment Requisitions
- Invoices
- Trends
- Procurement

Contracts

Let's look at the first three categories first since they are the most complex. Following is a table of the columns associated with these categories. Understand that the terminology used here is the standard out of the box terminology of PCM and may not match what has been set up in your organization. The third contract type (Custom) can be turned on or off using the Project Settings. It can be used for a variety of types as it has its own set of columns in the Cost Worksheet. The Custom contract type can be used in the Change Management module; however, it utilizes the Commitment tab, which requires the user to understand exactly what category the change is related. The following tables show various columns on the Cost Worksheet starting with the Cost Code itself.

The first table shows all the columns used by each of the three contract categories:

Cost Worksheet Columns

Cost Code	Original	Approved Revisions	Revised	Pending Revisions	Estimated Revisions	Adjustments	Projected

The columns listed above are affected by the Contracts, Purchase Orders, or any Change Document modules. Let's look at specific definitions of what document type can be posted to which column.

The Original Column

Cost Code	Original	Approved Revisions	Revised	Pending Revisions	Estimated Revisions	Adjustments	Projected
	Money distributed to Cost Codes from the Contracts modules are automatically posted to this column. Money can also be posted here from the Change Management module						

The **Original** column is used for money distributed from any of the Contract modules. If a Commitment contract is added under the Contracts – Committed module and the money is distributed to various Cost Codes (rows), the column used is the **Original Commitment** column in the worksheet. It's the same with the Contracts – Budgeted and Contracts – Custom modules. The Purchase Order module is posted to the Commitments category.

Money can also be posted to this column for Budget and Commitment contracts from the Change Management module where a phase has been assigned this column. This is not a typical practice as the **Original** column should be unchangeable from the values on the original contract.

The Approved Column

Cost Code	Original	Approved Revisions	Revised	Pending Revisions	Estimated Revisions	Adjustments	Projected
		Money distributed to Cost Codes from the Change Order module are automatically posted to this column if the change order document is *Approved*					

The **Approved Revisions** column is used for money distributed from the Change Order module. If a Change Order is added under the Change Order module against a commitment contract and the money is distributed to various Cost Codes (rows), and the Change Order has been approved, the money on this document is posted to the **Approved Commitment Revisions** column in the worksheet. We will discuss what happens prior to approval later.

The Revised Column

Cost Code	Original	Approved Revisions	Revised	Pending Revisions	Estimated Revisions	Adjustments	Projected
			This column is a computed column. This column is the sum of the Original and Approved Revisions columns on Cost Worksheet. Money can not be posted to this column from any document in PCM				

The **Revised** column is a computed column adding the original money and the approved money. Money cannot be distributed to this column from any document in PCM.

The Pending Changes Column

Cost Code	Original	Approved Revisions	Revised	Pending Revisions	Estimated Revisions	Adjustments	Projected

There are various ways that money can be posted to this column. (1) Unapproved Change Order, (2) Proposal documents, (3) Change Management documents assigned to the Pending column

The **Pending Revisions** column can be populated by several document types as follows:

- **Change Orders**: Prior to approving the Change Order document, all money associated with the Change Order document created from the Change Orders module from the point of creation will be posted to the **Pending Changes** column.
- **Change Management**: These are documents associated with a change management process where the change phase is associated with the **Pending** column. This can be from the Proposal module or the Change Order module.
- **Proposals**: These are documents created in the Proposals module either through the Change Management module or directly from the module itself.

The Estimated Changes Column

Cost Code	Original	Approved Revisions	Revised	Pending Revisions	Estimated Revisions	Adjustments	Projected

Documents associated with a Change Management process where the phase is assigned to this column. This can be a Proposal or Change Order type document

The **Estimated Revisions** column is populated from phases in Change Management that have been assigned to distribute money to this column (more on the reasons for assigning this column in *Chapter 9, The Only Constant Is Change*).

The Adjustment Column

Cost Code	Original	Approved Revisions	Revised	Pending Revisions	Estimated Revisions	Adjustments	Projected
	Documents associated with a Change Management process where the phase is assigned to this column. This can be a Proposal or Change Order type document						

The **Adjustment** column is populated from phases in Change Management that have been assigned to distribute money to this column (more on the reasons for assigning this column in *Chapter 11, Reading your Crystal Ball*).

The Projected Column

Cost Code	Original	Approved Revisions	Revised	Pending Revisions	Estimated Revisions	Adjustments	Projected
	This is a computed column. This is the sum of the Revised, Pending, Estimated, and Adjustments columns on the Cost Worksheet						

The **Projected** column is a computed column of all columns associated with a category. This column is very powerful in understanding the potential cost at completion of this Cost Code.

Actuals

There are two columns that are associated with actual cost documents in PCM. The modules that affect these columns are as follows:

- Payment Requisitions
- Invoices

These columns are the **Actuals Received** and **Actuals Issued** columns. These column names can be confusing and should be considered for change during implementation. This is the way you could look at what money these columns include.

- **Actuals Received**: This column holds money where you have received a Payment Requisition or Invoice to be paid *by* you. This also includes the Custom category.

- **Actuals Issued**: This column holds money where you have issued a Payment Requisition or Invoice to be paid *to* you.

As Payment Requisitions or Invoices are being entered and the money distributed to Cost Codes, this money will be placed in one of these two columns depending on the contract relationship associated with these documents. Be aware that money is placed into these columns as soon as it is entered into Payment Requisitions or Invoices regardless of approval or certification.

Procurement

There are many columns relating to the Procurement module. This book does not go into details of the Procurement module. The column names related to Procurement are as follows:

- Procurement Estimate
- Original Estimate
- Estimate Accuracy
- Estimated Gross Profit
- Buyout
- Purchasing Buyout

Variances

There are many Variance columns that are computed columns. These columns show the variance (or difference) between other columns on the worksheet, as follows.

- **Original Variance**: The Original Budget minus the Original Commitment

- **Approved Variance**: The Revised Budget minus the Revised Commitment

- **Pending Variance**: The (Revised Budget plus Pending Budget Revisions) minus (Revised Commitment plus Pending Commitment)

- **Projected Variance**: The Projected Budget minus the Projected Commitment

These columns are very powerful to help analyze relationships between the Budget category and the Commitment category.

Miscellaneous

There are a few miscellaneous columns as follows that are worth noting so you understand what the numbers mean:

- **Budget Percent**: This represents the percentage of the Actuals Issued column of the Revised Budget column for that Cost Code.

- **Commitment Percentage**: This represents the percentage of the Actuals Received column of the Revised Commitment column for that Cost Code.

- **Planned to Commit**: This is the planned expenditure for the Cost Code. This value can only be populated from the Details tab of the Cost Code. It is also used for an estimators value of the Cost Code.

Drilling down to the detail

The beauty of the Cost Worksheet is the ability to quickly review what documents have had an effect on which column on the worksheet. Look at the Cost Worksheet as a ten-thousand foot view of the money on your project. There is a lot of information that can be gleaned from this high-level review especially if you are using layouts properly. If you see some numbers that need further review, then drilling down to the detail directly from the Cost Worksheet is quite simple.

To drill down to the detail, click on the Cost Code. This will bring up a new page with tabs for the different categories. Click on the tab you wish to review and the grid shows all the documents where some or all the money has been posted to this Cost Code.

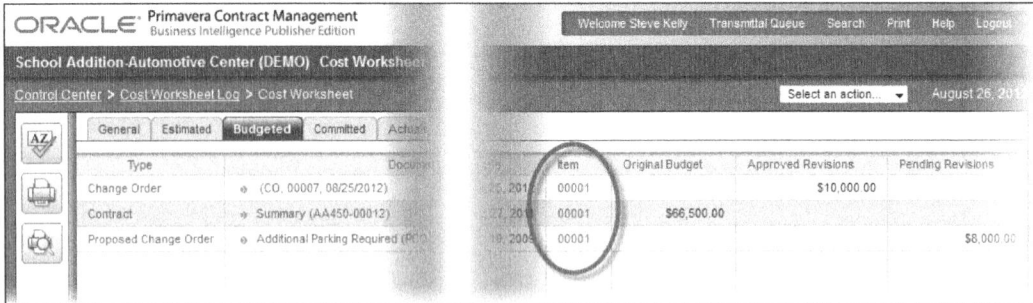

This page shows all columns affected by the selected category, with the rows representing each document and the corresponding value from that document that affects the selected Cost Code on the Cost Worksheet.

From this page you can click on the link under the **Item** column (as shown in the previous screenshot) to open the actual document that the row represents.

Summary

Understanding the concepts in this chapter is key to understanding how the money flows within PCM. Take the time to review this information so the other chapters on changes, payments, and forecasting make more sense. The ability to have all aspects of the money on your project accessible from one module is extremely powerful and should be one of the modules that you refer to on a regular basis.

The next chapter will discuss one of the most complex modules within PCM, the Change Management module. The combination of this chapter and the next couple of them are the basis for all aspects of managing project costs, which is at the heart of PCM.

The Only Constant Is Change

9

Changes to a project are inevitable. This chapter is all about managing changes against your contracts. Understanding the risk and what phase you are on during the change process is imperative. As multiple people are responsible for various parts of the change, you need a secure system in place where the users in all roles on your project can perform their jobs and give management a succinct understanding of their position on each change. Change can incorporate money and/or time and can either increase or decrease the contract value. The change documents in PCM are the only method that should be used to change your contract value. All contract types in PCM have the ability to be changed through the change process. The change process works hand in hand with contracts and the Cost Worksheet. In the previous chapter, you learned about the various columns on the Cost Worksheet. Many of those columns relate to various change documents processed in PCM through Change Management. The Change Management module is not a document creation module like Proposals or Contracts; it is a collection of all change documents related to a specific defined change of scope.

Understanding the process

Every organization has a change process in one way or another. The procedure is different, document acronyms are different, the number of phases are different, the amount of details they record is different; there are many variations. However, somehow all companies get from the initiation of the change to the final step by means of a Change Order type document. Some companies simply write a Change Order document and manage all the estimating and negotiating in their heads or on a spreadsheet. PCM allows each organization to set up its own process of managing changes. It allows for a different process per project if the need arises or a set of document types for a specific project is utilized.

Look at the change management process as a matrix. The rows are the contracts and contract types, and the columns are the phases. The rows are broken into two contract types: Budget and Commitment (the Custom category, if used in Change Management, also uses the Commitment type). PCM breaks the Change process into four phases as follows:

- Estimated
- Quoted
- Negotiated
- Final

Following is the Change Management matrix that we will walk through to understand each phase of each contract type. The acronyms and document types used may or may not be ones available out of the box but are used here to best portray exactly what each phase is related to. Yours can be different.

This matrix is depicted in the Change Management setup screen from the **Project Settings** window. The following screenshot shows the Budget section:

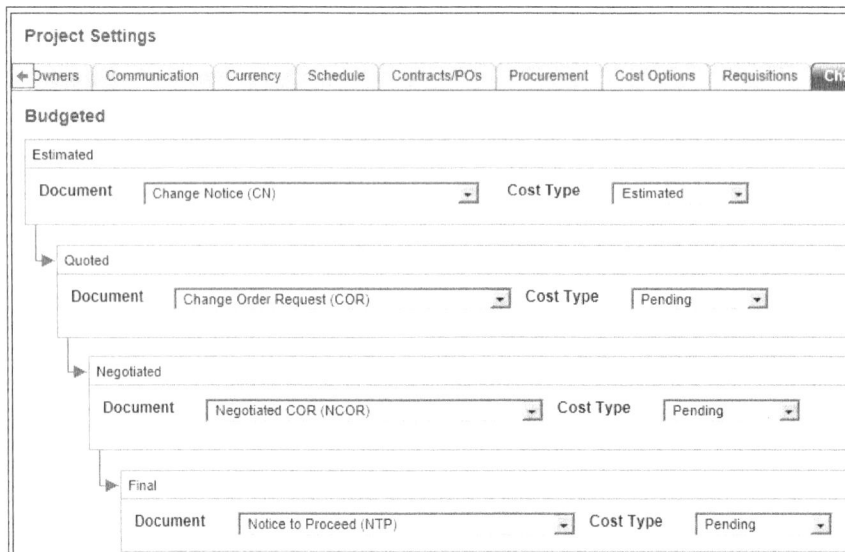

The following screenshot shows the Commitment section of the Change Management matrix setup in the **Project Settings**:

Each of these phases, for the two contract types, have the potential to record information in the form of a document or record in PCM. Some basic rules recommended about using Change Management in PCM are as follows:

- All phases do not have to be part of your organization's change management process.

- Use a different document acronym for each phase even though PCM allows a single acronym to be used in multiple phases. This way each acronym or document has a specific purpose.

Once the process is set up and implemented on your project:

- You do not have to use both contract types on every change
- You do not have to use all phases on every change
- You do not have to start at the first phase
- You do not have to end at the final phase

This allows the change management process to be completely flexible for your organization, specific project, or specific change within the project.

The number related to the Change Management record is significant. This is the Change Management Number or to better define its use you can use the acronym CCN for Change Control Number. This is the number that all correspondence related to this change needs to reference.

It is recommended that the actual forms printed or e-mailed from PCM relating to the change need to be changed in the report writer so that they clearly display the Change Control Number and state that correspondence relating to this change must include the Change Control Number (CCN). All the other documents that are going to be recorded into the Change Management record will have their own number based on their module. Using these numbers can be very confusing, so the CCN is the only number that should be used when relating to a change.

- Incorrect: "Here is our response to RFP number 46"
- Correct: "Here is our response to the RFP relating to CCN number 12"

The Change Management matrix needs to be defined for your organization and, if different, for your specific project. All parties involved need to understand the process of managing change to eliminate items falling through the cracks. Each of the cells in the matrix needs to be identified with a type of document. N/A (Not Applicable) is an acceptable entry in the matrix if your organization or your project will never be using that phase. Either way, each cell needs to be addressed. Even if you have a document for all or most of the cells in the matrix there needs to be room for flexibility to skip steps or start the change process at a different phase. That flexibility will be defined in your written procedures.

Documents and their associated acronyms are created at the database level, meaning that when added, they are available to be used on every project in the database. They are created in the **Document Setup** window available by right-clicking on the project tree and selecting **Document Setup** from the menu as shown in the following screenshot:

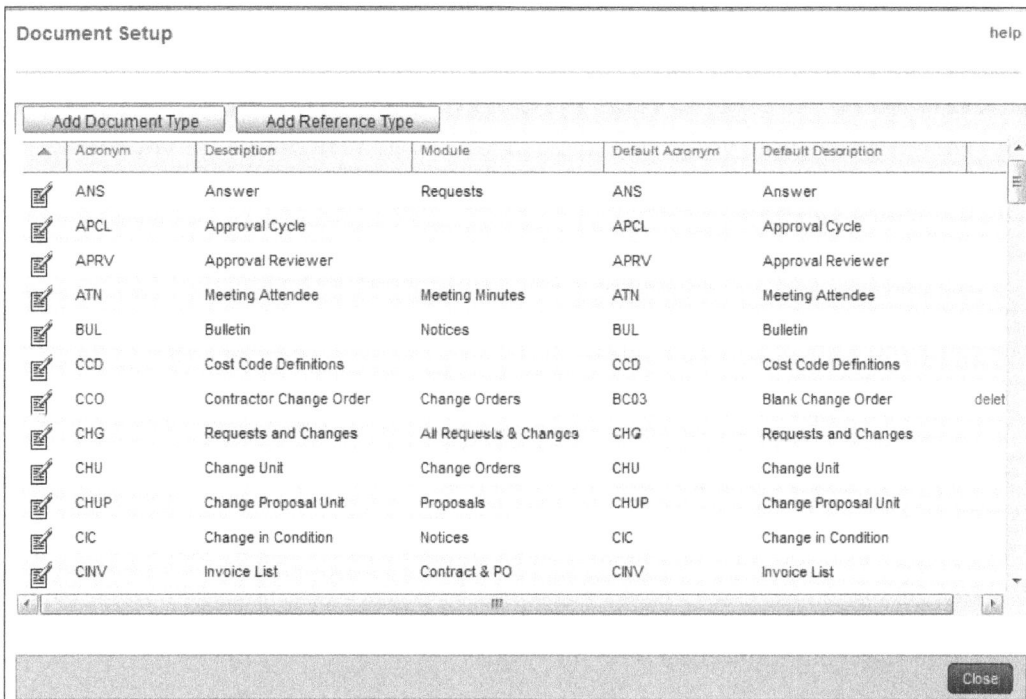

	Acronym	Description	Module	Default Acronym	Default Description	
	ANS	Answer	Requests	ANS	Answer	
	APCL	Approval Cycle		APCL	Approval Cycle	
	APRV	Approval Reviewer		APRV	Approval Reviewer	
	ATN	Meeting Attendee	Meeting Minutes	ATN	Meeting Attendee	
	BUL	Bulletin	Notices	BUL	Bulletin	
	CCD	Cost Code Definitions		CCD	Cost Code Definitions	
	CCO	Contractor Change Order	Change Orders	BCO3	Blank Change Order	delet
	CHG	Requests and Changes	All Requests & Changes	CHG	Requests and Changes	
	CHU	Change Unit	Change Orders	CHU	Change Unit	
	CHUP	Change Proposal Unit	Proposals	CHUP	Change Proposal Unit	
	CIC	Change in Condition	Notices	CIC	Change in Condition	
	CINV	Invoice List	Contract & PO	CINV	Invoice List	

Document Setup — help — Add Document Type — Add Reference Type — Close

What happens on the Cost Worksheet?

One of the features of the Change Management module is that the costs are automatically managed based on the workflow designed for the project. Since each category (Budget and Commitment) has four phases, there is the potential for having up to four individual documents under each phase with separate cost distribution information. The potential for doubling or tripling the monetary information on the Cost Worksheet would be high if not using the Change Management module. Using this module forces a workflow through the phases of the change. As a result, as each phase is added to the category, the previous phase is automatically closed and the money removed from the Cost Worksheet. There is no way to have two active documents populating the Cost Worksheet from one contract. The Budget category only allows a change to be associated with one Budget contract. The Commitment category allows unlimited commitment contracts to be associated with a change. Each of these commitment contracts can have only one active document within a particular change.

Example of a Change Management matrix

Following is an example of a potential Change Management matrix for you to review and make changes as your organization sees fit. This is just an example of how this matrix can be used, utilizing all phases with explanations. To help explain and understand this matrix, we have added not only an example document type and acronym but also who the document is sent *to* and who the document is sent *from*. This helps understand the flow of the documents in working through the matrix. The column the document is assigned on the Cost Worksheet is also discussed and recommended.

Budget Contract Estimated Phase

Once the change has been identified as a potential cost or time impact, there may be a requirement from the customer saying that he or she wishes to be notified of all potential changes that might affect the project. After the change has been initiated in the system and the Change Management started, this is the cell in the matrix that is entered to start communicating with the client.

Document Type

For the purposes of this example, let's call this document a **Change Notice** (**CN**). This document should be created as a Proposal type of document from the **Document Setup** window.

To and From

This document is *to* your customer and *from* your organization.

Cost Worksheet

The column to use on the Cost Worksheet should be the **Estimated** column. You will see that as we progress through this process, the **Estimated** column is exactly as it sounds. These are numbers, both on the Budget and Committed side of the Cost Worksheet, that are internal estimates with no paper backup to support the value from outside your organization.

	Estimated	Quoted	Negotiated	Final
Budget	Change Notice			
Commit #1				
Commit #2				
Commit...				

The following screenshot shows where this phase is started from within the Change Management module under the budget tab:

Estimated (CN)

Cost	$0.00
Time Change (days)	Start Estimated Phase
Document Date	

Quoted (COR)

Commitment Contract(s) Estimated Phase

The Estimated Phase on the commitment side of Change Management can be used as the "request for a price" document. The monetary values placed on these requests are your internal estimates of the contractor's portion of the change. This does not mean that those internal numbers will be communicated to the contractor. After the data is entered, the information can then be printed (except for your estimated value of the work) or e-mailed to the contractor(s) involved as a request for a price.

Document Type

Many organizations refer to this document as a **Request For Proposal** (RFP) or **Request For Quotation** (RFQ). This is the cell where the document is created to send out to the contractors requesting a price for their aspect of the change. There is an unlimited number of contractors that may be associated with a change and therefore you may send this request document to. Each contract represents a row in the commitment section of the matrix.

To and From

This document is *to* the contractor(s) and *from* your organization.

Cost Worksheet

The column to use on the Cost Worksheet should be the **Estimated** column just as with the Budget side. These are our internal estimates with no paper backup to support your estimate from outside of your organization.

	Estimated	Quoted	Negotiated	Final
Budget	Change Notice			
Commit #1	Request for Proposal			
Commit #2	Request for Proposal			
Commit ...	Request for Proposal			

The following screenshot shows many commitment contracts involved in this change. Each commitment contract has an RFP record associated with it, with most of them having an estimated cost of the RFP.

General	Status	Budget	Commitments	Remarks	Documents by Phase	Details	Issues	Attachments	Versions

Add   Add Multiple Estimates

▲	Include	Contract/PO	Estimated (RFP) Cost	Time	Date	Quoted Cost
🗋	✔	ACE Mason Contractors (AA450-00602)	$3,500.00	0	May 14, 2012	
🗋	✔	ACME General Contractors (DIRECT COSTS)	$1,000.00	0	May 14, 2012	
🗋	✔	Button Paint & Paper (AA450-00400)		0	May 14, 2012	
🗋	✔	Finish Ceilings, Inc. (AA450-01300)		0	May 14, 2012	
🗋	✔	Electrical Contractors (AA450-00001)	$750.00	0	May 14, 2012	
🗋	✔	Mechanical Contractors (AA450-00700)		0	May 14, 2012	

For the three commitment contracts with no money associated for the RFP in the previous screenshot, there is an RFP created but no line items have been added.

> Remember that all money entered in PCM will be distributed to the Cost Worksheet. Placing a value on this document is very important if you use the previous phase on the Budget side. If you enter a value on the CN but not here at the RFP phase, the Cost Worksheet will be out of balance and the variances will be misleading.

Commitment Contract(s) Quoted Phase

The Quoted Phase on the commitments section of the matrix is to record the quotes supplied by the contractors for their portion of the work. These quotes will be received into the project utilizing many different methods. The contractors can write on the RFP form and return it to you. This does not mean that you edit the RFP and enter the contractor's estimate. There must be a different record or document type to record this information in the Quoted Phase. You should never edit records that have been sent out.

Document Type

This is a cell where you record the information but probably will not print or e-mail a document from the system. For this exercise we will call this the **Quote** (**QTE**) and it will be a Proposal type document. As contractors respond to the RFP in the previous phase, their quote needs to be recorded on the same row in Change Management.

To and From

This document is *to* your organization and *from* the contractor(s).

Cost Worksheet

The column to use on the Cost Worksheet should be the **Pending** column. These are numbers, on the Commitment side of the Cost Worksheet, that now have external paper backup to support your estimate. This is not a duplication of the money; PCM will close the previous phase (RFP) and pull that money off the Cost Worksheet. More on the movement of the money on the Cost Worksheet and status later in this chapter.

	Estimated	Quoted	Negotiated	Final
Budget	Change Notice			
Commit #1	Request for Proposal	Quotation		
Commit #2	Request for Proposal	Quotation		
Commit...	Request for Proposal	Quotation		

The following screenshot shows the same commitment contracts used in the previous phase with some of the Quoted Phase populated where actual quotes have been received and entered. The **RFP** column represents your internal estimate for this change and the **QTE** column represents an actual quotation from your contractor(s).

If a contractor responds to your request (RFP) with no cost or time impact, a quote (QTE) is still created with a zero value. This shows that the contractor responded to the request.

Budget Contract Quoted Phase

This phase is your organization's proposal to the client. This is the document that compiles all the quotes from the various contractors and then includes your overhead and markup as a complete proposal to your client.

Document Type

For the purposes of this example let's call this document a **Change Order Request (COR)**. This document should be created as a Proposal type of document from the **Document Setup** window.

To and From

This document is *to* the client and *from* your organization.

Cost Worksheet

The column to use on the Cost Worksheet should be the **Pending** column.

	Estimated	Quoted	Negotiated	Final
Budget	Change Notice	Change Order Request		
Commit #1	Request for Proposal	Quotation		
Commit #2	Request for Proposal	Quotation		
Commit...	Request for Proposal	Quotation		

The easy method to create this phase is to use the **Copy Commitments to Budget** link. PCM will take all the active commitment documents for this Change Management and add them up with all the correct cost distributions. This phase also allows for you to use the Markup Matrix to calculate simple or more complex markups against the COR. The markup matrix is developed in **Project Settings**. The following image shows the window where you determine at what phase you want the commitment costs rolled up:

Copy Commitments to Budget

This will start a budgeted phase and copy the line items from included commitments (total value: $6,050.00) into the new budgeted document. It will not close or modify the commitments.

Select budgeted phase to start:

- ○ Estimated   (Change Notice)
- ◉ Quoted   (Change Order Request)
- ○ Negotiated   (Negotiated COR)
- ○ Final   (Notice to Proceed)

☑ Apply markup to the new document

The Negotiated Phase

The Negotiated Phase is designed to record various rounds of negotiation either between your organization and your contractors (Commitment) or your organization and the customer (Budget). PCM allows negotiation with either or both at the same time. You may choose to negotiate with your contractors before coming up with a new proposal value. You may negotiate with your customer first and then go back to your contractors and negotiate their quotes. PCM will record this phase either way. The use of the Negotiated Phase is to not change or edit the original quote. You could negotiate with your contractors before copying commitments to budget as described previously. You may use this phase to record all rounds of negotiation or just the final negotiated value.

Budget Contract Negotiated Phase

This is the negotiation you have had with your customer whether it is an interim round or the final round of the negotiations.

> PCM allows for unlimited rounds of negotiation. Each round will be stored and recorded as a different document in PCM for this change.

Document Type

For the purposes of this example let's call this document a **Negotiated Change Order Request** (NCOR). This document should be created as a Proposal type of document from the **Document Setup** window.

To and From

This document is *to* the client and *from* your organization. (If your customer sends you a counter proposal then the *to* and *from* are reversed.)

Cost Worksheet

The column to use on the Cost Worksheet should be the **Pending** column.

	Estimated	Quoted	Negotiated	Final
Budget	Change Notice	Change Order Request	Negotiated Change Order Request	
Commit #1	Request for Proposal	Quotation		
Commit #2	Request for Proposal	Quotation		
Commit...	Request for Proposal	Quotation		

The following screenshot shows the first three phases in the budget category with the button to start the Negotiated Phase:

You can also populate this phase using the **Copy Commitments to Budget** button.

Commitment Contract Negotiated Phase

This represents the negotiations you have with your contractors whether it is an interim round or the final round of the negotiations.

Document Type

For the purposes of this example let's call this document a **Negotiated Quote** (**NQTE**). This document should be created as a Proposal type of document from the **Document Setup** window.

To and From

This document is *to* the contractor and *from* your organization. (If the contractor sends you a counter proposal then the *to* and *from* are reversed.)

Cost Worksheet

The column to use on the Cost Worksheet should be the **Pending** column.

Change Management Matrix

	Estimated	Quoted	Negotiated	Final
Budget	Change Notice	Change Order Request	Negotiated Change Order Request	
Commit#1	Request for Proposal	Quotation	Neg. Quotation	
Commit#2	Request for Proposal	Quotation	Neg. Quotation	
Commit...	Request for Proposal	Quotation	Neg. Quotation	

Control Center > Change Management Log > Change Management   Select an action

General | Status | Budget | Commitments | Remarks | Documents by Phase | Details | Issues | Attachments | Versions

Add Add Multiple Estimates   Total Included Commitments: $5,300.00 Copy Commitments to

Include	Contract/PO	Estimated (RFP) Cost	Time	Date	Quoted (QTE) Cost	Time	Date	Negotiated (NQTE) Cost	Time
✓	ACE Mason Contractors (AA450-00602)	$3,500.00	0	May 14, 2012	$3,750.00	0	May 14, 2012	$3,550.00	0
✓	ACME General Contractors (DIRECT COSTS)	$1,900.00	0	May 14, 2012	$2,750.00	0	May 14, 2012	$2,200.00	0
✓	Button Paint & Paper (AA450-00400)	$0.00	0	May 14, 2012	$450.00	0	May 14, 2012	$450.00	0
✓	Finish Ceilings, Inc. (AA450-01300)		0	May 14, 2012					
✓	Electrical Contractors (AA450-00001)	$750.00	0	May 14, 2012	$0.00	0	May 14, 2012		
✓	Mechanical Contractors (AA450-00700)		0	May 14, 2012					

The Final Phase

The Final Phase can be used for the absolute final change document such as the **Change Order (CO)**. It also can be used for a document that represents that the change has been officially approved but will be rolled into an official Change Order at a later date. This process is where you collect multiple changes into one Change Order. The official change process and workflow is typically determined by the organization or by the project team.

Budget Contract Final Phase

This phase is the approval to proceed with the change and adjust the contract as directed by the change

Document Type

For the purposes of this example let's call this document a **Notice to Proceed** (NTP). This document should be created as a Change Order type of document from the **Document Setup** window. Use the Change Order type so that this document is in the Change Orders module rather than the Proposals module.

To and From

This document is *to* your organization and *from* the client even though your organization will most likely prepare the document for signature.

Cost Worksheet

The column to use on the Cost Worksheet should be the **Pending** column. The money will stay in the **Pending** column even though it is an officially approved document.

PCM does not allow the collection of changes into a Change Order if the documents are approved. You should never approve these NTP documents as they will not be available for collection in the next phase. If you want to approve them to place the money in the **Approved** column on the Cost Worksheet, they must be unapproved prior to collecting to the final Change Order in the next phase.

	Estimated	Quoted	Negotiated	Final
Budget	Change Notice	Change Order Request	Negotiated Change Order Request	Notice to Proceed
Commit #1	Request for Proposal	Quotation	Neg. Quotation	
Commit #2	Request for Proposal	Quotation	Neg. Quotation	
Commit ...	Request for Proposal	Quotation	Neg. Quotation	

The following screenshot shows all four phases of the Budget category with the Final Phase finished:

Estimated (CN)	
Cost	$5,250.00
Time Change (days)	0
Document Date	May 14, 2012

↝ Change in Tile (00001, 5/14/12, ACME General Contractors)

Quoted (COR)	
Cost	$6,957.50
Time Change (days)	0
Document Date	May 14, 2012

↝ Change in Tile (00001, 5/14/12, ACME General Contractors)

Negotiated (NCOR)	
Cost	$6,095.00
Time Change (days)	0
Document Date	May 14, 2012

↝ Change in Tile (00001, 5/14/12, ACME General Contractors)

Final (NTP)	
Cost	$6,095.00
Time Change (days)	0
Document Date	May 14, 2012

↝ Change in Tile (00001, 5/14/12, ACME General Contractors)

Commitment Contract Final Phase

This phase is the same as the budget side except this category is associated with your contractors

Document Type

For the purposes of this example let's call this document a **Contractor Notice to Proceed** (CNTP). This document should be created as a Change Order type of document from the **Document Setup** window. Use the Change Order type so that this document is in the Change Orders module rather than the Proposals module.

To and From

This document is *to* the contractor(s) and *from* your organization.

Cost Worksheet

The column to use on the Cost Worksheet should be the **Pending** column. The money will stay in the **Pending** column even though it is an officially approved document. (See the note on the Budget Final Phase mentioned previously.)

	Estimated	Quoted	Negotiated	Final
Budget	Change Notice	Change Order Request	Negotiated Change Order Request	Notice to Proceed
Commit #1	Request for Proposal	Quotation	Neg. Quotation	Contractor NTP
Commit #2	Request for Proposal	Quotation	Neg. Quotation	Contractor NTP
Commit ...	Request for Proposal	Quotation	Neg. Quotation	Contractor NTP

The following screenshot shows the Commitment category with the Final Phase entered for three of the commitment contracts:

Budget Contract Beyond Final Phase

If you want to use the Final Phase as a Notice to Proceed type document, you will still need an official legal Change Order against the contract. Usually there is a regular interval of time when Change Orders are created, perhaps once a month. This is where all of the currently available NTPs need to be collected into an official Change Order that truly changes the contract value. This Change Order document will be created from the Change Order module and the NTPs will be collected into that Change Order.

Document Type

For the purposes of this example let's call this document a Change Order (CO). This document should be created as a Change Order type of document from the **Document Setup window**.

To and From

This document is *to* your organization and *from* the client even though your organization will be creating the document.

Cost Worksheet

The column to use on the Cost Worksheet will be the **Approved** column. The money will be placed here as soon as the Change Order is approved.

Commitment Contract Beyond Final Phase

This is the same as the Budget side except this is with your subcontractors.

Document Type

For the purposes of this example let's call this document a Subcontractor Change Order (SCO). This document should be created as a Change Order type of document from the **Document Setup** window.

To and From

This document is *to* the contractor(s) and *from* your organization.

Cost Worksheet

The column to use on the Cost Worksheet will be the **Approved** column. The money will be placed here as soon as the Subcontractor Change Order is approved.

Now you should have a completed Change Management matrix for your organization. This will be the template by which your organization will manage changes unless a specific project dictates otherwise.

Following a change

We can now Follow along a typical change and use the Change Management module and process defined previously. To fully utilize the change process in PCM we need to understand the **Issues** module.

Issues

The Issues module is used for many different reasons in PCM; one of them is managing changes. The Issues module is a very simple and yet underutilized module in PCM. The name can be misleading and many times the name of the Issues module is changed to "File Index" as it can replace the company's F:\ drive that stores all project related documents. This method is very prevalent in organizations but can be very unwieldy and potentially insecure.. This module acts like an electronic file cabinet. The following screenshot shows an example of an **Issues** register:

It is the only module in PCM where you can link records (documents) from every other module in PCM. It is then a collection or folder of all documents related to a topic in one place.

Seasoned managers in PCM will live in two out of the 31 modules in PCM; the **Cost Worksheet** and the **Issues** modules. From either of these two modules you can drill down into specific documents that need your attention. They both have the capability of viewing the project from a high level and drilling down to the detail; the Cost Worksheet relates to the money aspect of the project and the Issues module relates to documents or potential changes yet to be resolved.

Initiating the change

When a change is encountered, there is some event that initiates the change. There are various different initiators of change on your project. Some of them can be:

- Request for Information (RFI)
- Drawing Change
- Daily Diary
- Inspection Report
- Field Directive
- Site Instruction
- Meeting
- Letter
- E-mail

This is just a short list and your organization will have different terms for some of these items. Regardless of the document or setting, there is something that will initiate the change process on your project. Initiating the change process does not mean that it is absolutely a change or that there will be more or less time or money as a result. As soon as you think there is a *potential* for change on your project, you need to record it so it can be tracked and not fall between the cracks. Too many managers think that if they have many potential changes on their project it reflects poorly on them; this is not the case. Management would rather have you identify potential changes rather than just letting them slide and being blindsided when it is too late to recover.

Whatever the initiator is, it should be entered into PCM in one of the many modules. If it is an RFI sent in from a contractor then obviously that will be entered into the RFI module. Once that RFI is entered into the system and there is a potential for a time or cost impact as a result of the answer to that RFI, the change process needs to be initiated. The Change Management module is one aspect of processing the overall change, but there are others within PCM.

Once the change has been identified, an Issue needs to be created and linked to the initiating document. This is done through the **Issues** tab on that document. You should use some intelligence to the Issue numbering as well by placing a C in front of a sequential number. Assigning an Issue to the initiating document is important to establish a folder from the start of the change. Once this is done, that folder (or issue) will also be attached to the other change documents automatically. Following is a screenshot of an RFI linked to an Issue named **Glazed Facing Tile**:

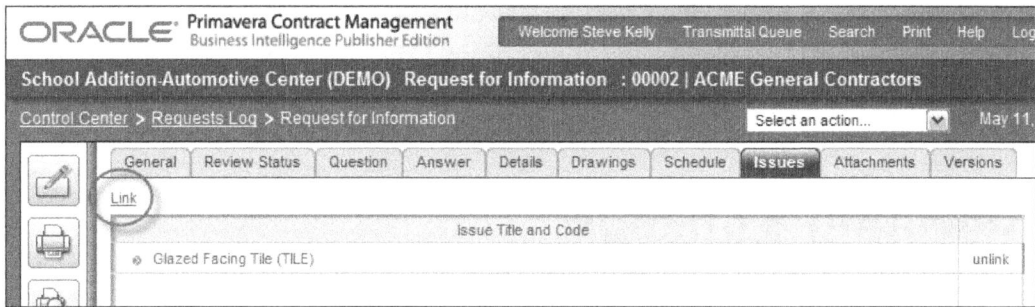

Almost every module in PCM can initiate the change management process that creates a record in the Change Management module. The Change Management module should be initiated from the initiating document. In our example of the RFI, click on **Initiate CM** from the **Select an Action** drop-down list of the initiating RFI. After you initiate Change Management, you should change the Change Management number to the same as the Change Issue number (in our example, C0001). This becomes your Change Control Number (CCN). PCM copies the title and remarks from the initiating document. It also keeps a link to the initiating document in the **Details** tab so you can always click on the link to review the initiating document. It also automatically links the Change Management record to the same Issue as the initiating document.

If you were to go to the **Issues** log and open **Issue C0001** you would find the initiating document and the Change Management record.

Now you can walk through the Change Management matrix as required on both the Commitment and Budget sides as necessary.

> If this is an internal change, there will be no information regarding the Budget side of the change. Just follow the matrix without using the **Budget** tab.

As documents are created as a result of starting a phase, the previous phase document is closed automatically and the money from that previous document is removed from the Cost Worksheet. This is important as you do not want multiple documents in different phases referencing the same contract affecting your Cost Worksheet. The current active document/phase for a contract row within the matrix is the only document that is affecting the Cost Worksheet. All the previous phases for that row, however, are still available for review.

At any time you can review the Cost Worksheet to see the stage of all potential changes on your project. Review the values in the **Estimated** versus **Pending** versus **Approved** columns. If you want to review specific numbers on the Cost Worksheet, click on the Cost Code and review the documents that affect that number.

Rejecting a change

As the change progresses through the procedure, there may be an instance when the customer decides that they do not want the change after all. You do not want to delete all the work you have already done and the communication that has occurred between the different parties. The way to reject a change completely is to change the status of the Change Management record to **Rejected**. Once this is done, all documents created from Change Management will automatically close and all the money related to this change will be removed from the Cost Worksheet. However, none of the documents or related costing will be deleted and you can always go back to this change for reference.

Types of changes

All kinds of changes can and should be recorded in the Change Management module. Some of them are listed as follows:

- **Change requested by the customer to add or deduct scope from his project**: In this case you will use both sides of the Change Management (Budget and Commitment) and most of the phases as required.

- **Missing scope from your original estimate**: If your organization missed some scope and therefore the change being tracked is considered "in the scope of the project," you will only use the commitment side of Change Management. You will be requesting your contractors to price out some scope that will increase their contract to accommodate for the scope.

- **Back charge to a contractor**: A back charge will involve one or more contractors such that you will deduct money from one contractor and add it to another or to your contingency. This can end up being a net-zero change.

- **Time and material change**: Time and material changes can also be tracked in the Change Management module.

Summary

Change is inevitable. Your organization needs to be prepared for multiple changes on a project. To prepare yourself, you need a process and a Change Management matrix defined so all changes follow the same process. These changes can range from having very small impact to very large impact. Tracking the changes in a consistent manner will allow management to understand any potential risk on the project and put a plan in place to help mitigate that risk.

We have reviewed the contracts and contract changes; the next chapter will discuss the method and process for getting paid and for paying contractors.

10
Time to Get Paid

Most contractors do not want to run a "not for profit" business even though
sometimes it feels that way. Most owners want to be sure and only pay for the value
of the work accomplished every month. How do we keep track of all the different
areas of work and their progress to properly get paid by the owner and to properly
pay the contractors we have working for us? PCM has a module for this process.
This is the module that ties all of it together and manages the amount of money
that gets deposited in your account.

There are two modules that manage payments on a project: the **Payment
Requisitions** module and the **Invoices** section of the Contracts module. Each
of these modules posts money to the Cost Worksheet on one of two columns
depending on the type of Contract with which they are connected.

Cost Worksheet and payments

The Cost Worksheet has two columns in which the two payments modules will post money. The following screenshot shows the Cost Worksheet out of the box with these two columns:

- **Actuals Issued**: This is the column where payments that are related to a Budget Contract are posted
- **Actuals Received**: This is the column where payments that are related to a Commitment Contract or Purchase Order are posted

The naming of these columns seems to be misleading as you would think that the **Actuals Received** column is the column where money that has been *received* has been posted, but that is incorrect. Think of it as the column where money is posted when a Payment Requisition has been received. If you receive a Payment Certificate from a contractor, you will be *paying* them money. The opposite is true for the **Actuals Issued** column. This is the column where money is posted from a Payment Requisition that you are *issuing* out to your client. This is money that you will be *receiving*. The best way to not make these columns so confusing would be to change the name of the columns using the **Customized Text** feature to best meet the needs of your organization.

Money is posted to these columns as soon as it is posted as a payment in PCM using either of these two modules. This does not mean that the Payment Certificate is approved or accepted; it is just entered in PCM.

> As soon as money is entered into a Payment Certificate or Invoice, it is posted to the Cost Worksheet. There is no specific differentiation between *pending* payments and *actual* payments on the Cost Worksheet.

For a Payment Requisition document, money is posted in the **Completed and Stored to Date** column of the Payment Requisition Pay Item as shown in the following screenshot:

For an Invoice record, the **Amount Billed** column (shown in the following screenshot) is the field that appears on the Cost Worksheet:

Be sure to note that the Invoices module posts money to the Cost Worksheet from the **Amount Billed** field, not the **Amount Paid** field.

When a Contract or Purchase Order is created in PCM, both options for payments are available to be picked for the first payment, **Invoices** and **Payment Requisitions**:

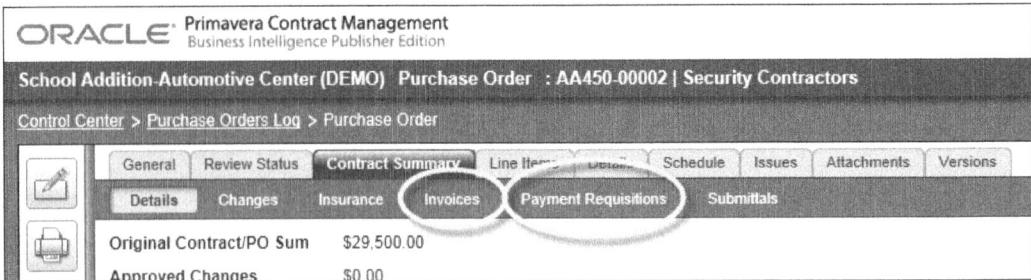

Once a payment type is selected (**Invoices** or **Payment Requisitions**), that is the only payment type that can be used for that Contract or Purchase Order. You cannot mix and match between **Payment Requisitions** and **Invoices**.

There are various parties on a project that need to track payments. These modules are designed to manage any of them as they relate to your company. As an example, if you are the General Contractor on a project, you manage the amount of money you will be paid by the owner and the amount of money you will be paying each subcontractor or supplier.

Difference between Payment Requisitions and Invoices

While both of these methods track money movement between two parties, they are quite different in their complexity. The decision to use one or the other depends on many factors, such as:

- Are payments made as a one-time single payment or a monthly draw?
- Is retention involved in the Contract?
- Will you allow your contractors in your system to post amounts?
- Is there an approval cycle involved in the payments?
- Are unit price items involved?

The **Payment Requisition** module is much more complex than the **Invoices** module. **Payment Requisitions** is designed for the monthly payments against a Contract where retention is typically involved. You can track and pay based on an unlimited number of **Payment Requisition Line Items** (Pay Items). These Pay Items can be lump sum or unit price items. Unit price items can then be managed using the **Materials** module to track materials received on a project and post against a Pay Item on the **Payment Requisition**.

The **Invoices** section of the **Contract Summary** is designed as a single payment against a Contract or Purchase Order with a single amount. There are no Pay Items or unit pricing involved in Invoices.

Both modules assign payments to Cost Codes on the Cost Worksheet. By default, PCM assumes that the Cost Codes assigned to the Contract or Purchase Order will be used; however, this can be changed.

Setting up the Payment Certificates module

As with many of the other modules in PCM, proper setup of this module is key to a smooth operation of receiving and sending payments during the project. During the Contract negotiations process, typically the various Pay Items are discussed and agreed upon prior to signing the Contract. Once the Pay Items are agreed upon, the Payment Requisitions module can be set up.

Cost options

There are various settings available to the user prior to creating the first Payment Requisition. These settings are available to be changed at the Project Settings level and then again at the Contract or Purchase Order level. Any changes made at the Project level will only affect any contracts created *after* the setting has been changed. Any changes made at the Contract level will only affect Requisitions created *after* the settings have been changed.

Project Settings

The Project Settings are available by a right-click on the project from the **Project Tree**. These options are available under the **Requisitions** tab. When a Contract is created in PCM, these options are inherited and assigned to that Contract. The options can be changed using the **Requisitions** tab of **Project Settings** as long as the options are changed before creating or generating the Contract or Purchase Order. If a Contract is already created, these settings can only be changed by selecting the **Cost Options** from that Contract prior to creating or generating your first Payment Requisition. The following screenshot shows the **Project Settings** screen with the **Requisitions** options:

Project Settings

| ← | Key Parties | Default Owners | Communication | Currency | Schedule | Contracts/POs | Procurement | Cost Options | **Requisitions** | → |

Schedule of Values

☑ Allow the Value in Completed and Stored to Date (column G) To Exceed the Line Item's Budget in Scheduled Value(column C)

When generating a new application, Primavera should do the following with values in Materials Presently Stored (column F):

◉ Leave Them in the Same Column in the New Application

○ Move Them to Previous Applications (column D) in the New Application

When adding new line items to the Schedule of Values:

Start with this line item: *   0000010

Increment line items by: *   10

Retainage Calculation

◉ Calculate the Retainage Using Summary Percentages

☑ % of Completed Work Until Work Is: 50.00   Complete

☑ % of Stored Materials

○ Enter Retainage on Line Items

On new line items, set the retainage rate (column I) to: 9.00

○ Enter Total Retainage in the Requisition Summary

Tax Calculation

◉ Enter the Tax to Date Amount in the Requisition Summary

○ Enter the Tax Rate on Line Items (column J) and Let Primavera Calculate the Tax to Date Amount

* Required

Let's look at what these settings mean:

1. **Allow the Value in Completed and Stored to Date To Exceed the Line Item's Budget in Scheduled Value**: When checked, the value in Completed and Stored to Date (column G) is allowed to exceed the value in Scheduled Value (column C). When unchecked, the value in column G cannot exceed the value in column C as shown in the screenshot below. Basically, if checked, this means you can bill for more than your current value for this Pay Item.

Scheduled Value (C)	Previous Applications (D)	This Period (E)	Materials Presently Stored, Not in D or E (F)	Completed and Stored to Date,D+E+F (G)
$240,000.00	$240,000.00	$0.00	$0.00	$240,000.00
$274,264.12	$274,264.12	$0.00	$0.00	$274,264.12

2. The next question is a radio button to select one or the other option relating to the Materials Presently Stored (column F). You can choose to keep them in column F or move them to Previous Applications (column D).

3. The next two fields determine how the Pay Items are to be numbered. The first entry is to place the starting number of the Pay Items and the next field is to place the increment number. It is a good idea to place leading zeros on your starting number. Be sure to increment by enough numbers in case you need to add numbers in the future or add blank lines (see next section). PCM orders the Pay Items by this number so planning ahead is important and there is no utility to mass update or renumber this field.

4. There are three ways to calculate the retainage on the project:

    ° Calculate the retainage at the master or summary level where all the Pay Items are added together and you have one retainage percentage applied. There are two subdecisions to make with this option: To calculate the retainage up to a certain percentage of completion and whether to calculate retainage on Stored Materials.

    ° You can calculate retention at each line item. This way a line item can have a different retainage percentage than other line items.

    ° Simply enter a value (not percentage) on the **Requisition Summary** tab.

5. There are two options for entering taxes on the project: To enter the value (not percentage) or to enter a tax percentage at the line item level.

> Note that retainage calculations affect tax calculations. Retainage will be held on pre-taxed values of the Pay Item.

Cost Settings (Contract level)

The **Cost Settings** can be selected from the **Select an Action** drop-down list of the Contract or Purchase Order. These options must be changed prior to creating or generating a Payment Requisition. The settings are the same as the Project Settings except for the first setting, which affects Invoices only.

Cost Options

Contract/Purchase Orders

☑ Do Not Allow Invoices to Exceed Revised Contract/Purchase Order Value

---

Creating the Payment Requisition template

It is good practice to prepare a template of how the Payment Requisition is going to look prior to creating your first requisition. Creating a template is a good way to start and confirm the Pay Items for the Contract while not having any effect on the first Payment Requisition. This can be numbered "0000". Payment Requisitions can be created using the Payment Requisitions module; however, they are easily created from the Contract or Purchase Order to which they are related. Creating from the Contract or Purchase Order will assign a payment item to each line item. Open the Contract and select **Generate** from the **Select an Action** drop-down list. The following window is displayed to answer a few questions. The first question is all that matters when creating the template. Be sure and select a date that is before the expected first payment date from this contractor or supplier.

Generate Requisition

This will create a new Requisition for this Purchase Order.

Period To *   Jan 1, 2012

Link the new Requisition to the same Issues as the original?
◉ yes   ○ no

Link the new Requisition to the same Attachments as the original?
◉ yes   ○ no

When you generate the Payment Requisition from the Contract or Purchase Order, PCM will take any line items you have and create Pay Items from them using the numbering method chosen in the Cost Options. PCM will also assign the same Cost Code(s) for each Pay Item as the ones assigned in the contract line item. (You only have one chance to pull in original lines from the Contract.)

> This Pay Item list can be completely changed or summarized. The Pay Items do not have to match or line up with the line items in the Contract as long as the total Scheduled Value of all the Pay Items adds up to the Contract value.

The following screenshot shows a Payment Requisition **Schedule of Values** tab. Circled is the total of the Scheduled Value amount from all Pay Items. This should equal the Contract value.

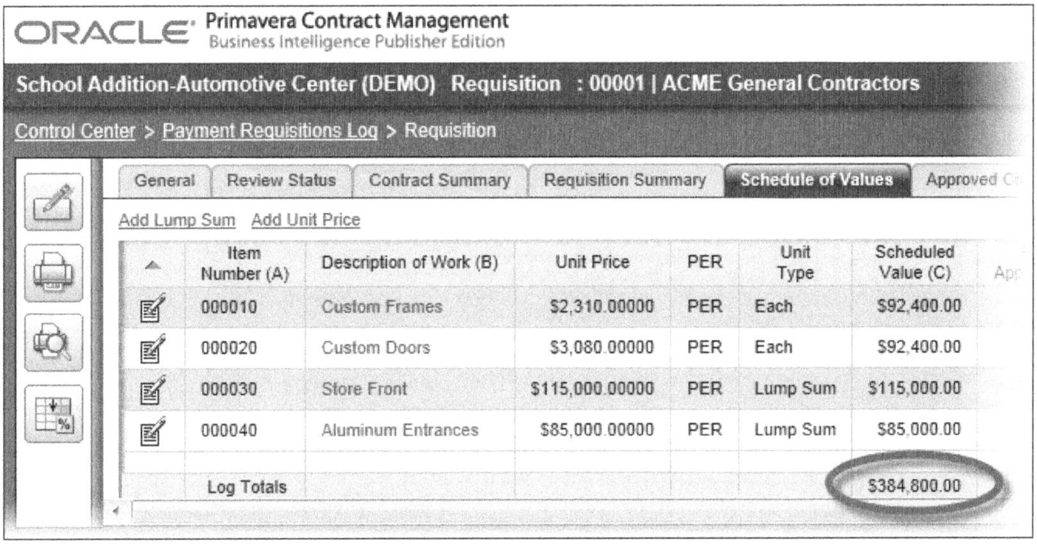

Following is a screenshot of the **Contract Summary** tab of the Payment Requisition with the **Original Contract Sum** circled. This is the value that should match the circled number in the previous screenshot.

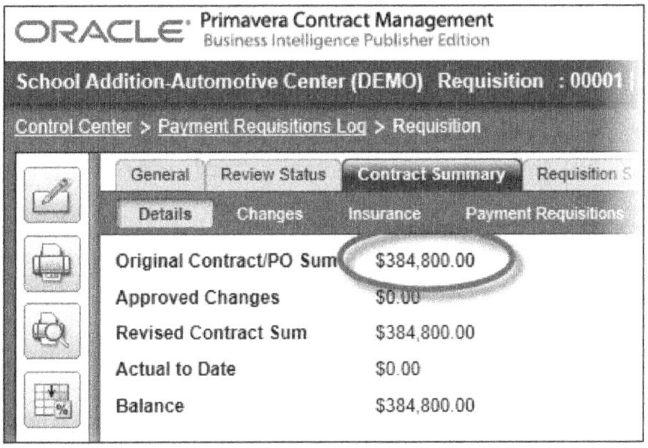

Adjusting and adding Pay Items

Pay Items can be added or removed as required from the **Schedule of Values** tab. The Pay Item Number can be changed to place it in a different order. The Schedule of Values will be ordered by the Pay Item Number for any added subtotals to work properly.

There are five types of line items that can be added to the Schedule of Values. The first two listed as follows are accessed from links at the top left of the **Schedule of Values** tab of **Payment Requisition**. The last three are available from the **More commands** drop-down list available at the upper right of **Schedule of Values** as shown in the following screenshot:

- **Add Lump Sum**: These Pay Items can be added as required with the Item Number, Description, Scheduled Value, and cost distribution.

- **Add Unit Price**: These Pay Items can be added as required with the Item Number, Description, Quantity of Units, Unit Price, and Cost Distribution.

- **Add Subtotal**: This item type will create a subtotal of all the previous Pay Items up to the previous subtotal or the top of the Pay Item list.

- **Add Header**: This item type is strictly for adding a header to a group of Pay Items. There is no monetary information stored with this item type.

- **Add Blank Row**: This item type is strictly for adding a blank row in the list of Pay Items. There is no monetary information stored with this item type.

See the following example of how these items can be used:

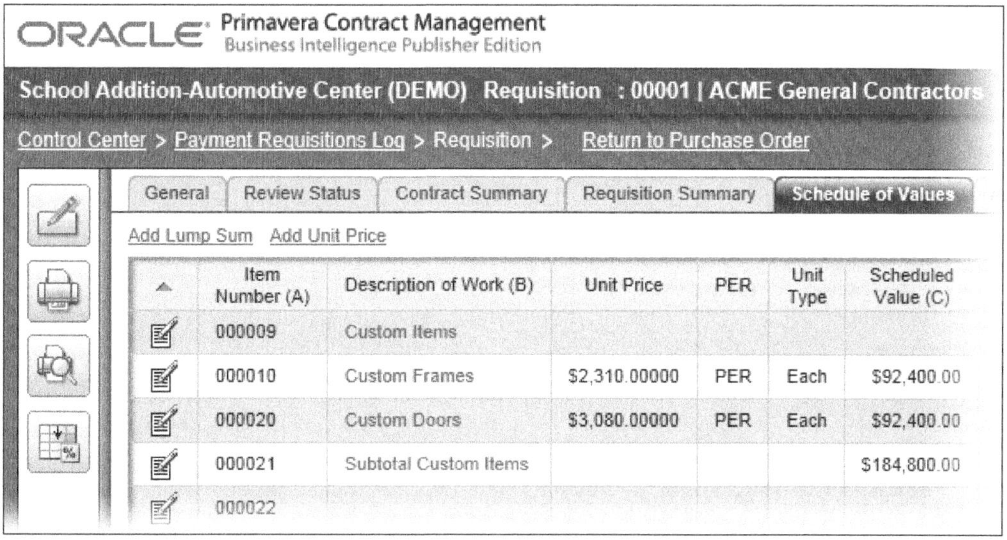

Notice that Pay Items **000009**, **000021**, and **000022** were added but nothing was added to **Schedule of Values** for the Contract; **000009** is a **header**, **000021** is a subtotal, and **000022** is a blank line.

Processing payments

Once the template is complete, it is time to generate your first Payment Requisition either to be paid or to pay your contractors. The payment process becomes simple after the template is created.

To create a monthly Payment Requisition, open the previous month (if this is the first month, open the template) and click on **Generate Document** from the **Select an Action** drop-down list. Answer the questions on the window that is displayed and a new requisition will be created with any money in the **This Period** column (E) moved to the **Previous Periods** column (D).

After the Requisition is created, you can get Change Orders relating to this Contract that have not yet been associated with a previous Requisition by clicking on **Get Approved Changes** from the **More Commands** drop-down list:

Get Approved Changes

Contract	Summary (AA450-00012)
To	ACME General Contractors
From	Philadelphia County

Create line items for

◉ Total Change amount   ◯ Each line item

[Select All]   [Unselect All]

Select	Title	Number	Date	Total Cost	Approved Date 1	Approved Date 2
☐		00007	Aug 25, 2012	$1,000,001.00	Aug 7, 2012	Aug 7, 2012
☐	NTP # 1	00001	May 16, 2012	$10,000.00	May 17, 2012	May 17, 2012

 These changes will come into this Requisition as new Pay Items with a leading "C" character. These Pay Item Numbers can be changed/edited as needed.

The Requisition is created but each Pay Item needs to be progressed as agreed by the parties involved. There are multiple ways to accomplish this. Select **Update This Period** from the **Select an Action** drop-down list (or click on the **Update This Period** button on the left) to display a grid of all Pay Items for this Requisition. You can progress either the percent complete of the Pay Item and the amount will be calculated or enter the actual billed value of the item and the percentage will be calculated.

After the values are agreed, this Requisition must be certified to lock the values. This is done on the **Review Status** tab.

> Any value entered in Column (G) for each Pay Item will be posted to the associated Cost Codes of that Pay Item on the Cost Worksheet.

Invoices

If the Invoice method is selected, the entry is quite simple. Multiple Invoices can be added to a Contract. The information stored for the Invoice is limited:

- Invoice Number
- Invoice Date
- Title
- Amount Billed
- Amount Paid
- Payment Date
- Check Number

Following is a screenshot of the **Invoice** data entry screen. The value is posted to the Cost Worksheet.

Invoice				
General	Contract Details	Costing	File Index No	Attachments

Number	00001
Date	Nov 23, 2012
Title	Lockers, Identification, & Fire Extinguishers
Ball in Court	ACME General Contractors Charlie Jones
Priority	Normal ▾
Status	New Item ▾
Amount Billed ($)	50,000.00
Amount Paid ($)	50,000.00
Payment Date	
Check Number	
Activity ID	

Summary

Getting paid keeps the doors of your business open. Make sure you are getting paid what you deserve. If you are an owner, be sure to pay only what is earned by your contractors. Managing the Contracts and changes is great as long as you are getting paid properly and on time.

In the next chapter we will be looking at forecasting and predicting the future using the Cost Worksheet.

11
Reading your Crystal Ball

There are times when having a crystal ball would surely be nice. When we are making picks for the stock market or picks for a horse race it would be nice to have a crystal ball; but it would really be nice to know what the future holds for our projects. PCM has a way to look into the future and see what the potential for your project or a portion of your project is. PCM can look at existing information along with external information you may have and let you know what the expected outcome could be monetarily. Like any other system, the adage "Garbage in, Garbage Out" is true when looking at the future since it is so dependent on past information.

How is this possible

If you apply all the principles discussed in this book relating to monetary information, PCM actually knows quite a bit about your project. If it is a large project, it is practically impossible for you to keep all the issues and potential changes in your head. Even if you are Superman and have a mind that can remember everything, the problem is that it is in your head and not available for others to review or analyze. We have been looking at PCM as a data capture tool for the most part ... up till now. Now is the time to take that information and have the system *be* that crystal ball.

A database system like PCM stores vast amounts of information with the capability of quick and easy retrieval. PCM is also a browser-based application, which means it can be accessed from any device that has a browser (for the most part). This power allows anyone with access to review the project from several different perspectives and locations in real time. No more waiting for a spreadsheet to be finished on Bob's computer. Therefore, forecasting can be done any time, in real time.

Forecasting

The term forecasting has been used as a method for predicting the future of a project. It looks at current information and then with some input from the project management team as well as some smoke and mirrors, there is a number that represents the "Estimated Cost at Completion" of the project. This is an extremely oversimplified definition of forecasting but you get the point. Every company has its own way to look into the future; from a S.W.A.G. (if you don't know this acronym, ask someone on the project – they will know) to an extremely sophisticated spreadsheet that has all kinds of bells and whistles to help a user understand all the elements. These spreadsheets can be filled with different colors and groupings and buttons, you name it. Most organizations require a forecast be performed once a month. These forecasts many times take up to three weeks to compile as all kinds of information needs to be retrieved, verified, and entered into this fancy spreadsheet. Then it takes several meetings to justify any overages or underages and perhaps a bit of fudging is applied to make the numbers look a bit better.

> Remember what was said about spreadsheets in *Chapter 4, The Almighty Spreadsheet*. The good thing about spreadsheets is you can make them look exactly the way you want. The bad thing about spreadsheets is you can make them look exactly the way you want.

If it takes three weeks to compile, the users only have one week of reprieve before they have to start the process all over again. It also means that some of the data on the spreadsheet is several weeks old by the time it is presented to the management. Some of the information comes from accounting, which by design is a history recording tool, so this information is old.

Even the best of management and their staff using the best tools possible can only come up with a number that is close or has an average level of reliability. With all the information you need at your fingertips and the information in PCM, which is real time (as long as the other roles are doing their jobs), you can push that button that gives you the most up-to-date and reliable information on the project. Let's look at what PCM already knows:

- Budget information
- Budget changes
- Original Contract and Purchase Order values
- Approved Contract and PO changes
- Pending changes (both budget and committed)

- Estimated changes (changes not yet processed from the contractors)
- Actual amounts paid to contractors and suppliers
- Actual amounts paid to the project

All these items are broken down to the Cost Code level on the Cost Worksheet. The Cost Code is the lowest common denominator for tracking all things monetary.

There is only one piece missing in our puzzle to create an accurate forecast. This is the information that management knows but PCM would have no reason to know. All of the information on the previous list is provided as a result of something being entered into PCM. The reason it has been entered is that there is an event that triggered those entries. For example, a contractor was selected and therefore a Contract was written, signed, and entered into PCM. What PCM does not know is what the management team knows about the pulse of the project; what they know about potential cost increases or decreases.

Trends

PCM has a module to allow management to provide this information to the Cost Worksheet; it is the Trends module. We have also provided a column on both the budget and commitment side of the Worksheet for this information to be placed. This column is the **Adjustments** column. The following screenshot shows how a **Trend** document is allocated to the proper Cost Worksheet column:

Any information that management wants to enter, that they know, will affect the project monetarily needs to be entered in the Trends module. Most of the time there are only costs entered that affect the commitment side of the spreadsheet. In other words; the project management team may know about some upcoming extra costs or cost savings that PCM would have no way of knowing. They also may know about a particular unapproved Change Order in the system that will not get approved. These are the things that needs to get entered on a monthly basis and allows the project management input into the bottom line of the project. For each of these changes, there is room for text to be added to explain why they are adding or deducting money.

The Trends module holds temporary information during the course of the project. As trends are or are not realized, the trend document will go away. By the end of the project there should be no trends affecting the Cost Worksheet.

The Cost Worksheet is the tool that is used to manage the forecast. The commitment side is the money that will be spent on the project. The **Commitment Adjustments** column is where you need to post money using the Trends module as the money that project management will enter.

Let's look at the columns again in the Cost Worksheet:

- **A (Original commitment)**: Money is posted here from the signed Contract and Purchase Order values.

- **B (Approved Commitment Revisions)**: Money is posted here from approved changes against any of the approved Contracts or Purchase Orders.

- **A+B**: This is the sum of column A and B that provides the reader the current Contract values including approved changes.

- **C (Pending Commitment Revisions)**: Money is posted here from the change documents that have paper backup from the contractor or supplier and is still in progress (not yet approved).

- **D (Estimated Commitment Revisions)**: Money is posted here from the change documents that are your estimates of potential changes.

- **A+B+C+D+E**: This is the sum of all these columns including the **Commitment Adjustments** column. This becomes the "Estimated Cost at Completion" value for this Cost Code. The total of this column is the potential Estimated Cost at Completion of the project.

- **E (Commitment Adjustments)**: This is the column that needs to be set when creating a trend. This is where the management team will enter values by Cost Code of information they know that PCM does not.

The only column in the above equation that is not populated by a contractual document (contracts or changes) is **Commitment Adjustments**. So this is the only column that the management team has access to change that affects the Estimated Cost at Completion number. All the other columns are populated by contractual documents in the system.

An example of how this is used is if there is a change in process that management knows will not be approved by the client. This can be "trended out" of the **Projected Commitment** column which represents the Estimated Cost at Completion. Another is if there are some known time and cost extensions coming up that management knows about but PCM would have no changes in place yet to accomodate them.

This system is only as good as the expedience and accuracy of the information entered into PCM. This shows that PCM is very role based and that each role is usually very dependent on another role to complete his task before he can work on his own. Part of the training process requires users to understand this concept (see *Chapter 16, Where Do We Go from Here*).

Seeing into the future is actually quite easy when a system like this is followed and managed. At any time during the month a "current status" report can be run to show where the forecast sits at any point in time.

Summary

This chapter is where it all comes together monetarily. Since you are putting all the other information into the system to provide proper documents and so on (contracts, change documents, Payment Requisitions), it makes sense to take the extra step and be able to provide an incredible amount of information easily and on time without taking three weeks to compile. Management will still have the ability to "hide" money in locations they know they will need, but now they can place that money in those codes with confidence knowing all the other information. It is no longer a scientific guessing game.

In the next chapter we will change gears and look at how drawings are stored and managed for your project.

12
Managing Drawings

Drawings or technical documents form the foundation of any building project. They are the instructions on what the project will look like when it is finished as well as what types of materials will be used to get there. It can be extremely complex to understand and track changes to them. They have many dimensions to explain exactly what size and location to build the item they reference. Some projects have tens of thousands of these documents or more. Managing all these documents and their revisions can be a daunting task, not counting the distribution of all these documents to the correct parties. At any time, PCM allows any user to view what the latest revision of a particular document is and the distribution of that revision (as well as all past revisions). Having this information can certainly be beneficial in a litigation case.

What are drawings

Through the years that PCM has been used, the Drawing modules has gone through many iterations. In the past, there was a complex wizard that allowed the user to use the Drawings modules to initiate change or become a result of a change, as well as having many other branches. It was extremely complex and was met with resistance from the user community. The **Drawings** and **Drawing Sets** modules are now designed specifically for documents that will potentially be revised and distributed to multiple parties. Typically, the drawings and specifications of a project are sometimes called technical documents. This module is best used after these drawings have been issued for construction. It is not typically used for design reviews prior to being issued for construction. It can be set up to monitor those as well, but the limited collaboration aspects of PCM limit the true design review comments as they would be visible to anyone assigned to the drawing. The "Issued for Construction" drawings are the turning point, as this is the complete set of drawings used to determine the cost of a project. Contractors use this set to estimate and negotiate their price for a project and the point that contracts are signed. There are many types of contracts that are different from this model; however, this is the simplest to understand and use as an example for this chapter.

Adding drawings to my project

Every sheet of the drawing list should be entered into PCM as a single drawing record. Any of these sheets can be revised so the need to track the revisions and therefore their distribution of that revision against that one sheet is important. Of course, when you are looking at potentially thousands of sheets or more, this may seem impossible. The following screenshot shows just one tab of the large amount of fields that can be entered when managing drawings:

At the beginning of the project, the objective is to just get the list in the system. All this information is not required initially; however, the more we can enter upfront the less we will need to enter at a later date. There are some fields that will be populated as the drawing is revised or distributed. There are several methods to add all the sheets of drawings to a project. This is another module where it takes time to enter the information upfront but during the course of the project, managing this information becomes much faster.

> No matter what method you use to populate the drawing register, be sure to enter an initial revision to each drawing. Drawings without a revision assigned will not be available to a Drawing Set explained later in this chapter.

One by one

One method to add drawings to PCM is by adding them one by one into the drawings module. This is ok for a few drawings but it can be very time consuming and hardly worth the effort for any more than a couple.

Import

PCM has a specific import structure for creating a CSV file in your spreadsheet to import multiple drawings at the same time. Not all fields are available for import using this method. Be sure to use the export function to get the specific fields and order of fields that can be imported, as shown in the following screenshot. When starting a project, this method is much quicker; however, with any CSV import you need to be sure that all the fields are in the exact spot with correct date formatting and so on. After a few tries you will get it.

Third-party import tools

There are other third-party import tools available, such as CMPlus, written by Pro Management Systems, Inc. (www.allthingscm.com). CMPlus allows you to import all fields for a drawing including all fields and custom fields in one or multiple revisions and including attachments to the drawing or revisions, all with one import CSV file. CMPlus also has a feature to add initial and additional revisions to drawings that are already entered into PCM. When there are tens of thousands of drawings to import, tools like this are extremely useful.

Whatever method you choose to enter these records it is important that this be done at the beginning of the project or as soon as you get the "Issued for Construction" set of drawings.

PCM only holds the records for tracking and managing the drawings; these are not the drawings themselves. The drawing files can be attached to these records if you want, but these files (unless simple PDFs) can be quite large and time consuming to attach.

> The CMPlus application mentioned previously also has the ability to import the attachment files if you are using the "file location" method of storing attachments.

Managing drawings

Entering the drawings into the system is only half the battle. The reason we enter them is to manage them and have the capability to understand each drawing's current revision and distribution at the click of a button. There are two main aspects of the Drawing module: revisions of the drawings and distribution of the drawings.

Revising drawings

A project wants all parties involved to be working from the same instruction set. Drawings are changed regularly as the job progresses, and there will be conflicts and items that need clarity. Revisions to drawings can be dramatic changes or just simple changes. If certain contractors are working from an old set of drawings, their information is outdated and they could be spending valuable time and money in the wrong place. It then can become a blame game, whether they were notified of the revision and when that notification was made.

It is recommended that any change to any drawings, either one drawing or many, be made through the Drawing Sets module. The Drawing Sets module is a way to perform a revision or distribution function to a grouping or set of drawings. This process forces all revisions to be made the same way regardless of complexity or quantity of drawings.

To register a revision to a set of drawings add a new Drawing Set and provide a Name, a Title and a Date. Then on the **Drawings in This Set** tab, click on the **Record** link as shown in the following screenshot:

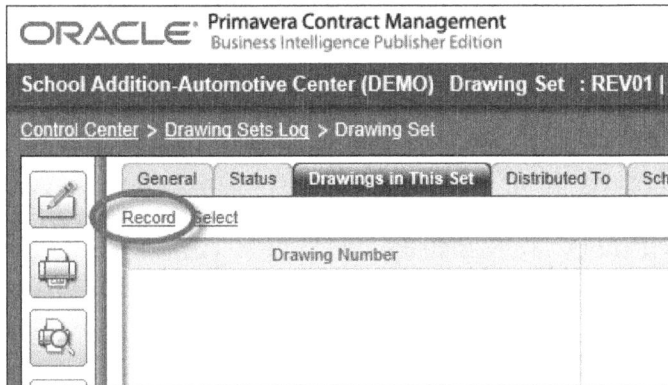

> To remember the difference between the **Record** and **Select** link on this tab, think of it this way: You are going to *Record* a Revision and *Select* for Distribution.

In the window shown in the previous screenshot, click on the **Select** link to select the drawings that are being revised in the following set:

For each drawing select the checkbox stating that it is a new revision and provide the revision details for each drawing.

> Remember that drawings cannot be placed in a set unless they have at least one revision assigned. This is by design in the application. Even if the drawing truly has no revisions, you will need to add one as Rev 0 or 0.0 so the system can then incorporate that drawing into sets. If you are creating a set and a drawing does not appear in the **Select** list, it does not have at least one revision associated with it.

After this is done, you will need to distribute these revised drawings to the proper parties. On the **Distribute To** tab of the set, you can click on the **Copy From Drawings** link. This is very powerful, as PCM will go to all previous distribution parties associated with any/all of the drawings in this current set and add them to the distribution list. There is no way a person can remember or know what drawings are in whose hands and what the latest revision is. This feature solves that problem. After PCM finds all the parties, the list can be modified by clicking on **Remove link** for contacts you do not want to distribute to, and by clicking on the **Select** button to add more contacts to the distribution list as shown in the following screenshot:

Add Distributions					help
Select		Sent Date Jul 17, 2012			
Distributed To	Distributed To Contact	Copies	Paper Size		
ACE Mason Contractors	Dave Barron	1	B (12 x 18 in.)	▼	remove
Standard Paving and Concrete, Inc.	Jim Wesley	2	D (24 x 36 in.)	▼	remove
Tri-State Steel	James Taylor	2	D (24 x 36 in.)	▼	remove
Stesson Industrials	Michael Austin	2	C (18 x 24 in.)	▼	remove
Moore Paving	John Kelly	2	D (24 x 36 in.)	▼	remove
Baines Steel	Helen Prugh	1	B (12 x 18 in.)	▼	remove
Adams Masonry	Greg Fox	1	B (12 x 18 in.)	▼	remove
Structure Inc.	Samual Adamson	2	D (24 x 36 in.)	▼	remove

This distribution list then goes to the Transmittal Queue where a transmittal can be processed for delivery or recording the delivery. The Transmittal Queue is discussed later in this chapter.

Distributing drawings

There may not be a revision but you still may need to distribute drawings to one or more parties on your project. The Drawing Sets module is the place to create and manage this distribution.

To select the drawings that you want to distribute, create a new Drawing Set as described previously. After you create the set click on the **Select** link to select a list of drawings to be distributed. The following screenshot shows the **Select** link on the **Drawings in This Set** tab:

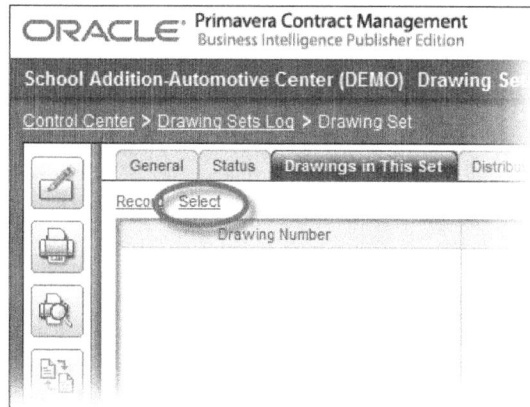

In the window that appears, click on the **select** link next to any drawing you want included in this set for distribution, as shown in the following screenshot:

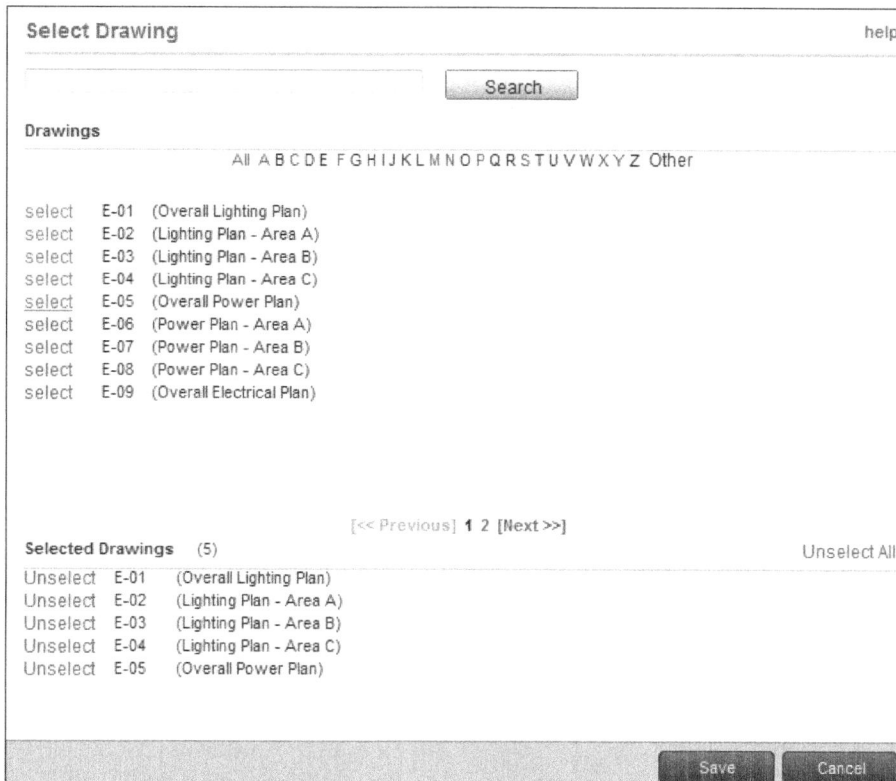

If you accidently select a drawing that you do not want in this list, click on the **Unselect** link next to that drawing.

This will also populate the transmittal queue for the possible creation of a transmittal.

Summary

As a result of managing all the revisions to all the drawings and specifications on your project and also distributing drawings using PCM, you have the power and ability to understand exactly what set of drawings you and your contractors should be working on. There is now a record of the dates of the revisions and the dates of distribution of those revisions to all parties involved. There should be no misunderstanding regarding pricing of changes and submission of submittals or even manufacturing parts for the project.

Knowing exactly what the status of drawings look like at any point in time on a project is required when the timing of revisions or distribution of those drawings is in question in any litigation that may arise as a result of sloppy distribution of that revision. When a change proposal comes through, the contractor should be able to tell you what revisions on what drawings were used to prepare his proposal. Let's all work off the same set of drawings.

In the next chapter we will look at Submittals, which may or may not include drawings.

13
Processing Submittals

It is hard to believe that most companies do not manage submittals but simply record history regarding submittals. What do I mean by record history? Recording history means that when a submittal comes in, they record the day it arrived. When they send it out for review and approval, they record the date they sent it. When it comes back from the approver they record the date it was returned and so on. If you are just going to record history, you may as well use a cheaper tool, like a spreadsheet.

Submittal overview

There are many ways to define a "submittal." As far as PCM is concerned, it is anything that requires an approval. This is a pretty broad description; let's narrow it down a bit. It is anything that is to be submitted to the project as a requirement of the drawings or specifications that must be "approved" before moving forward. This can include the following (although certainly not an exhaustive list):

- Shop drawings
- Cut sheets
- Samples
- MSDS sheets
- Closeout items

These are items that require approval prior to continuing on with the purchasing or fabrication of a particular item. This may seem unimportant; however, studies have shown that poor submittal processing and management play a key role in delays and added costs to a project. If a certain item cannot be ordered unless it is approved by the owner or engineer and if the approval is delayed for some reason, the item cannot be ordered. If the item cannot be ordered then of course it can't be delivered to the site for installation. If it is late being installed, it can delay other aspects of the project and so on. If you simply record history regarding submittals, you only have your memory to count on regarding when submittals need to be approved.

Concepts for submittal management

The concept of managing submittals relies on how the submittal register is set up. There are various ways to accomplish this. The level of detail of this register determines the level of detail for managing and monitoring your submittals. Each submittal record in PCM represents a single level of approval. For example, if you are entering submittals for the electrical package on a building, there are typically many fixtures that need to be approved. Cut sheets about each fixture need to be submitted. So the question is: do you enter a submittal for each fixture or do you enter one submittal called "fixtures"? Since each individual fixture can be rejected or accepted, the answer is that you should enter each fixture as its own submittal. There may be exceptions to this method but this is the general rule.

Each submittal is assigned a workflow that it will follow for the final approval. Following is the approval cycle of a submittal:

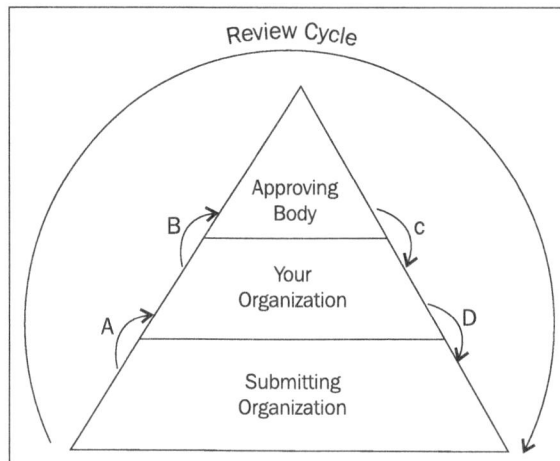

The various stages of the review cycle are as follows:

- **A** represents the date the submittal is received by the submittal coordinator of your company
- **B** represents the date the submittal was sent to the approving body
- **C** represents the date the submittal is returned back from the approving body to the submittal coordinator
- **D** represents the date the submittal was forwarded to the originating provider

This flow is called a **review cycle**. At the end of the review cycle there is a status associated with the submittal. If the status is not "approved," the process starts all over again and goes through the complete review cycle again. A submittal can go through this review cycle as many times as is required to achieve an "approved" status. Each of these steps in the workflow also represents a date. These dates are very important when it comes to managing the submittal register.

As the submittal progresses through the workflow, PCM knows who represents the Ball In Court or responsible party at all times. When the submittal is approved, the Ball In Court is removed from the submittal.

So far we are still only recording history, but we are recording all aspects of the submittal review cycle process. The proper way to manage the submittals is to know one key piece of information: when does the submittal need to be approved before its delay affects the schedule and therefore potentially results in additional cost as well? When you know this date, you can compare this with any of the current dates you are recording throughout the review cycle to see how much time you have left before a submittal will affect time and/or cost. Better yet, if we can assign the submittal to an activity in our schedule, that date will always be accurate depending on the movement of the schedule.

Multiple reviewers

Each submittal has an "approving body." This can be one person or many people that have approval rights to a submittal. PCM allows you to assign multiple reviewers to a submittal, which means that *all* the reviewers must approve the submittal for it to be approved. If one of the reviewers rejects the submittal, the submittal is rejected and needs a new review cycle.

PCM allows for all of this information to be entered and managed, but it all starts with proper setup and entry of the submittal register prior to the start of the project.

The submittal register

The proper way to manage submittals is with the submittal register. This is a list of *all* items that require approval on the project. This can be a long list. Like most other modules in PCM, the preparation of managing submittals will take the most time. Then the actual management of the submittals during the project will be very quick and easy.

At the start of a project, the entire list of submittals need to be entered into PCM. PCM has provided several ways to create this list to make this process as easy as possible, but it still will be time consuming. Before entering these submittals, there is some information you need to know.

Submittal setup

There is some setup that is required prior to entering submittals in the register. Under **Project Settings** there is a Submittal Coordinator that needs to be assigned under the **Key Parties** tab. When the project is set up, it is a required field but you may have the wrong person entered in that field. Verify that the person selected in the **Project Settings** is truly the person in your organization who is responsible as the "gatekeeper" in the management of submittals for your organization. PCM only allows one submittal coordinator per project. That is why we call them the gatekeeper. This is the person that then distributes the submittal to the appropriate individual if it is not himself.

Submittal packages

Submittal packages are a way to organize your list of submittals. There are various ways you can "group" or package your submittals.

Group by specification section

The most common way to group submittals is by the specification section, which is a dictionary available in PCM to be used by several modules. This way all submittals relating to electrical for example, will be in the same grouping. The package then takes on the spec section number and title.

Group by vendor

Another way to consider grouping your submittals is by the supplier or vendor. Since submittals usually arrive in a group from your vendor, you only need to open one package to manage these submittals. If a vendor is supplying materials across multiple spec sections, you would have to open those spec section packages and process each package. There are other fields within the submittal where you can place the spec section number if you need to report based on spec section.

The power of using packages goes far beyond just a way to organize your submittals. Using packages allows you to set up a workflow at the package level. It also allows for the creation of multiple submittals at one time, so when you create them they all inherit that package-defined workflow. Also, when managing submittals you can manage at the package level and have this information propagate down to the individual submittals.

Creating the submittal register can be done using the standard import procedure within PCM. You must create the import file exactly as required by the header. If you want to create the submittal register using the interface, you need to decide about how you will manage the packages. For the sake of example let's use the spec section concept of packages.

The third party product, CMPlus mentioned in the previous chapter also imports submittals with custom fields.

You create packages from the Submittal Packages module by providing a number and a title. Under the **Workflow Template** tab you design the workflow of all submittals that will be created under this package.

> If a submittal is created using a package, the workflow will inherit the workflow of the package but can be edited and changed after it is created.

This tab shows a graphical representation of how the submittal will work its way to the various parties. Any submittal generated from this package will inherit this workflow to save time in entering all this information for each submittal.

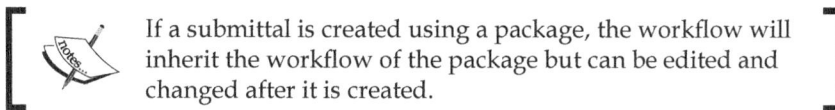

Under the **Submittals** tab you have two options: **Add a single submittal** and **Add Multiple Submittals**. Adding a single submittal just takes you to the Submittal module with the inherited information already populated. When you click on **Add Multiple Submittals** the window asks how many submittals you want to create as well as the starting number. PCM assumes you want to number with a PACKAGE – 001 format but this can be changed here.

This is the fastest way to create multiple submittals as much of the information is entered at the package level and then "copied" to as many submittals as you like. You will only have to enter the titles of the submittals as well as a category and type if required in the next window. When finished, PCM will automatically assign the status of "UnSubmitted" to each submittal. This tells you and PCM that the submittal has not been submitted by the first party in our workflow.

The next step in the setup of your submittal register is the most important if you want to manage your submits rather than record history. Each submittal has a **Required Finish** field. This field is the most important. The definition of this field is "The date that this submittal must be approved before it affects time or cost."

In other words, this submittal can go through as many review cycles as needed as long as it is approved by that date.

This date may be months into the future but now we have a benchmark to compare current date information against, to *manage* our submittals. Entering a date in this field can be done in four different ways:

- **Sledge hammer approach**: Simply type a date in this field.
- Use the **Schedule** tab as shown in the following screenshot and enter the start date of the activity where this item will be needed on the project. Then enter the Lead Times for some or all of the various categories. Once you click on the **Update from Lead Time** link this will automatically populate the required **Finish** date as well as all the other dates in the **Schedule** tab.

[PCM only manages calendar days. It has no concept of working days.]

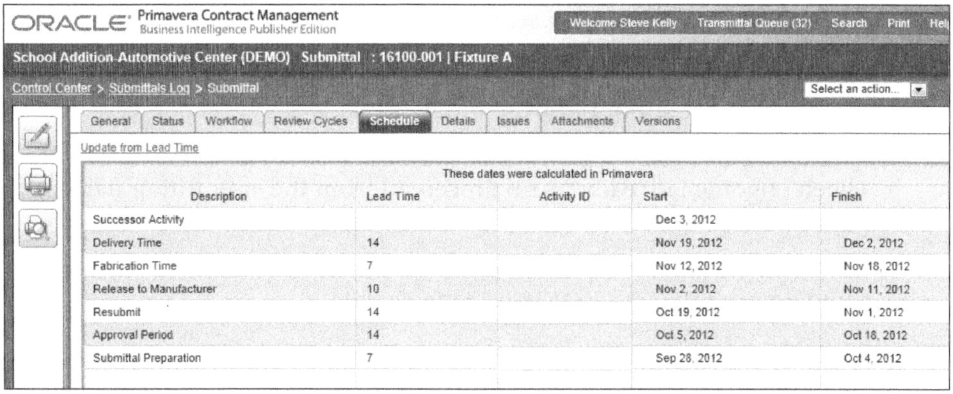

The following screenshot shows how the **Required Start** and **Required Finish** dates are populated from the dates on the **Schedule** tab:

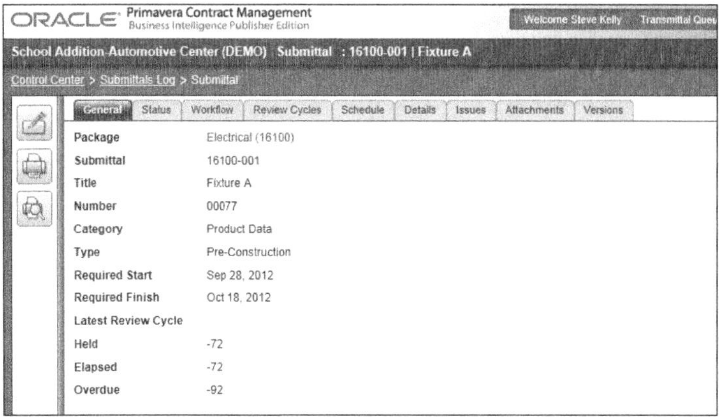

- **Link to P6 schedule**: If the project is properly linked to a P6 schedule, you can select the activity from a drop-down list where this item will be required on the site and then enter the Lead Times, similar to what we did in the previous option.

- **Import**: You can enter this date in the import file prior to importing into PCM.

PCM populates the **Required Start** date as well, using this method. This date represents the date that the submittal process must start before possibly affecting your schedule and cost (assuming that your lead times are correct).

You do not have to enter or manage every submittal to this level of detail but there are probably many submittals that are critical to your project where you want to know exactly where you stand.

There are some other interesting numbers on the **General** tab that are worth mentioning to help you manage your submittals:

- **Held**: This number represents the number of days that the current Ball In Court has held the submittal from today's date

- **Elapsed**: This number represents the number of days that the submittal has been ongoing since it was first received from the submitting party to today's date

- **Overdue**: This number represents the number of days that the submittals is past the Required Finish date from today's date

You can see that any one of these fields can help you understand the current status of a particular submittal. Many reports are available or can be created to present the submittals in a manner that allows you to see the submittals that demand your time; that is how you *manage* your submittals instead of simply recording history.

Managing submittals

Now that all your submittals are entered into PCM you can start to manage them. This process becomes much easier as all the expected submittals are already entered into PCM. Submittals can be processed individually or by the package. The package method is the easiest as the package will already filter the long list down to a manageable level.

Definitions of submittal progress dates are as follows:

- **Date Received**: This is the date on which the submittal was received from the submitting organization to your submittal coordinator

- **Date Sent**: This is the date that the submittal coordinator sends the submittal to the approving body
- **Date Returned**: This is the date when the approving body returns the submittal to the submittal coordinator
- **Date Forwarded**: This is the date that the submittal coordinator forwards the submittal to the submitting organization

When you receive the submittals from the submitting organization you open the package and click on **Update Package**. This way you can pick which of the submittals in the package they have submitted and enter the date on which the submittal was received.

The following screenshot shows how to select Submittals for update in a Package:

Update Submittals in a Package

Mark the checkboxes for all the Submittals you want to update

	Submittal No.	Title	Status	Latest Rev.
☑	16100-001	Fixture A	UnSubmitted	
☑	16100-002	Fixture B	UnSubmitted	
☑	16100-003	Fixture C	UnSubmitted	
☑	16100-004	Fixture D	UnSubmitted	
☑	16100-005	Fixture E	UnSubmitted	
☑	16100-006	Fixture F	UnSubmitted	
☐	16100-007	Switchgear	UnSubmitted	
☐	16100-008	Cable Tray	UnSubmitted	
☐	16100-009	Rough-In Boxes	UnSubmitted	
☐	16100-010	Disconnects	UnSubmitted	

There is no status yet so leave everything else blank.

PCM automatically knows that the submittal is no longer "UnSubmitted" as well as when to start the time clock for the Elapsed Time field.

Using our example of the electrical fixtures, if the electrician sends you a notebook of all the cut sheets for all the fixtures, it is easy to open the package and check all the fixture submittals and enter one date. Any attachments to submittals such as PDF files should be attached at the Review Cycle level during the review cycle. Only attach files to the submittal level once the submittal has been approved. This method will keep you from getting confused during the approval process.

The **Ball In Court** fields in the Submittals module is not editable by the user. This information is derived from the workflow and dates that have been entered into the workflow for each submittal.

When it is time to forward these fixture submittals to the approving body, you go through this process again by selecting all the fixture submittals from the package and only entering the Sent date. If you notice that one of the cut sheets is wrong and want to send this information back to the submitting organization, you can do this as well by only checking the problem submittal and only entering the Forwarded date and selecting Rejected for the status.

Since all this information is entered in real time, the reporting from this module is also in real time. You can run a report at any time to see the status of your submittals on the project. This is a perfect place to use alerts to show when submittals should begin to be placed on your radar as the Required Finish date gets closer and closer.

When the submittal has gone through the review cycle and gets approved, the Ball In Court is dropped off and the submittal is considered finished. If a review cycle is rejected, a new review cycle needs to be started and the process is started all over again until it is approved.

Transmittals

When you enter a date in the Sent or Forwarded fields, PCM assumes you would like to prepare a transmittal to go along with the submittal since it is being sent from your organization to someone else. This information automatically populates the Transmittal Queue.

Summary

Truly managing submittals is just as important as managing changes on your project. If you do not manage submittals properly, you will most likely have more changes and those changes will not be in your favor. PCM allows for easy management of submittals if you take the time for proper setup at the beginning of the project.

The next chapter is all about the various documents created out in the field and how to use PCM to manage this information.

14
Out in the Field

There are many modules within PCM that are designed to be used in the field and are not necessarily related to cost directly. These include RFIs, Meeting Minutes, Daily Reports, and Punch List. There are other modules as well, but, they are fairly self-explanatory and not in need of explanation at this level. The modules in this chapter are designed to keep the record of progress and communication in one location. The additional benefit is that users with access to the system can review any items where they may be responsible.

- **The Request for Information (RFI) module**: This module is the most collaborative module in PCM and is specifically designed for a question and response
- **The Meeting Minute module**: This module not only records information discussed in a meeting but also allows you to manage that information and prepare agendas
- **The Daily Reports module**: This module can record all detailed information happening on the project on a daily basis
- **The Punch List module**: This module manages all the items that need attention prior to completion of the contract or project

Let's look at each of these modules in more detail.

Request for Information

This module is one of the staples of the construction industry. This is a module for questions and answers. When you have a question that needs to be asked, you fill in the appropriate fields and then wait for the answer. The answering party then fills in the answer and you can review the answer, all in one place. There needs to be an ordered and structured location to manage these questions. Parties are contractually bound to ask and answer questions in the correct format and timeframe. There are some basic problems in the workforce with respect to RFIs however.

- **E-mail is too easy**: E-mail has taken the place of an official RFI in many cases. This is a terrible mistake as there are typically no defined procedures for e-mail communication. A person tends to feel that e-mail communication is informal and therefore would not be responsible for the content of the e-mail in a litigation case. There is so much information that can be inferred with an e-mail. E-mail is also not secure. If an individual wishes to delete an e-mail, he or she has that capability. Some organizations are using **Microsoft Exchange** to monitor the deletion of e-mails but they are few and far between. Organizations should require that all official project related communication must happen through a project level e-mail address such as *myproject@mycompany.com*. PCM has a process that will retrieve those e-mails and automatically populate them in the Correspondence Received module. Someone will need to be responsible to monitor this module but at least all communication gets placed in one location. Even with this functionality, all questions should be placed in the RFI module. Leave e-mails to ask about who is going to win the big game this weekend.

- **The answering party does not have access to PCM**: It is easy to create RFIs and e-mail the PDF of the form to the answering party, but if they do not have access to PCM, they will have to somehow communicate the answer back and it needs to be placed in the answer field of the RFI. This is not very efficient and therefore gets skipped.

- **The question is being asked while not close to a computer or PCM**: Many times questions are brought up during a walk-through of the project. Currently there is no mobile solution from Oracle to quickly record these questions. There are some third-party products available that may be a solution for this, so the questions can get asked via an e-mail from your smartphone or tablet.

RFIs are typically where change management is initiated. When the answer is reviewed, there may be a potential time or cost impact associated with the answer. PCM allows for initiating change management from the RFI itself (as well as many other modules). This keeps a trail of communication that can be followed long after the change is administered. You need to be able to retrieve what initiated that change.

There are times when the answering party just does not answer the question with enough detail and the question needs to be revised or asked again. PCM allows the *daisy chaining* of RFIs by using the **Generate** command from the **Select an Action** drop-down list. When you generate a new RFI from an existing one PCM keeps the originating RFI information in the new RFI. This way if the question is rewritten or asked four or five times, there is a chain of RFIs that can be reviewed quickly. Deleting or rewriting the data in an RFI is bad practice. There always needs to be a record of information that was entered or sent out. Organizations are way too dependent on fancy numbering systems and insist that the daisy chain of RFIs needs similar numbering.

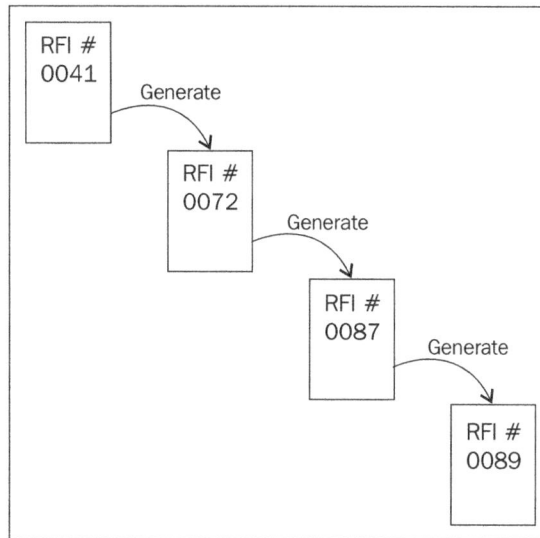

With a database system where records are linked together, the sequential numbering system is not necessary. The application allows you to jump back to the previous RFI and with some fairly simple reporting have a report that shows the daisy chaining of multiple RFIs. Don't get caught up in the "old school" way of thinking with fancy numbering systems.

In the following screenshot, the RFI number 00016 was generated from RFI 00004. In the **Details** tab of the RFI, the **Reference** field is the referencing RFI. When you are in View mode, this field becomes a link that you can click to go back to the originating document.

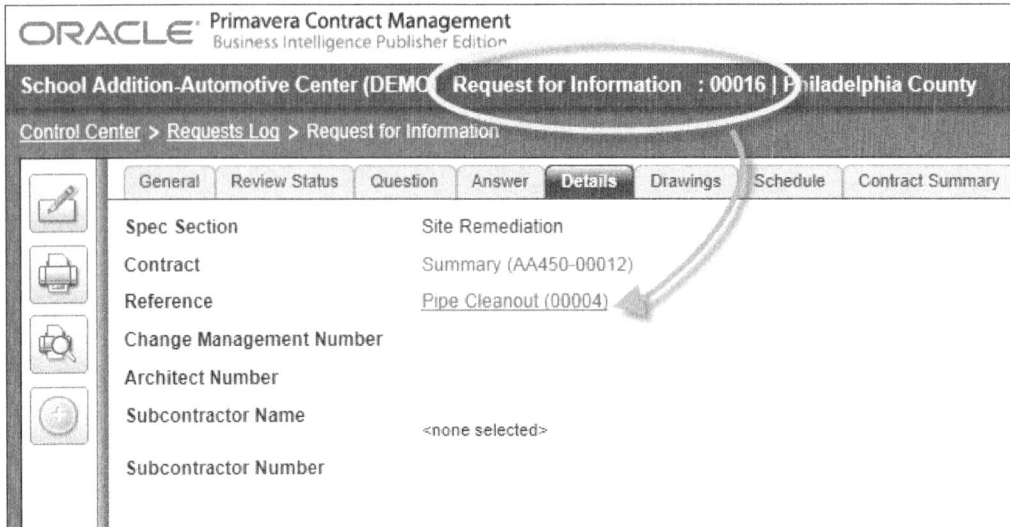

Meeting Minutes

Recording and managing what is said in meetings can keep you out of court or at least help you win your case. Many organizations say that they do not want to get "stuck" keeping the weekly progress meeting minutes. This is crazy. They should all be jumping at the opportunity to be the one that records the information stated in a meeting. They would be the ones that write the story of what was said. Few people like meetings and even fewer like taking the meeting minutes, but when you are in a litigation case, wouldn't it be great if the court was reading your "story" of what was said in a meeting rather than the person sitting at the other table in the courtroom?

Many organizations insist on extremely fancy formatting of the minutes so they can look pretty. Not sure if this is to distract from the fact that they have very little substance in the verbiage, but arbitrators could care less how fancy they look; they are looking at the content. PCM doesn't have the fanciest looking minutes available but having all documented information in *your* system of what was said in a meeting is very important. PCM even has the capability to lock these meetings once everyone agrees to them at the next meeting.

Each business item listed stands on its own. If that business item is discussed over several meetings, that discussion is added to the *same* business item. Each business item can be assigned one responsible party to complete the item and a Due date for the item. The status of the items changes as time moves on.

The following screenshot shows the list of business items within a meeting including the assignment of responsibility and Due dates:

When the business item is first introduced, it is assigned the status of **New**. In subsequent meetings, that business item is assigned the status of **Old** until it is completed when it gets assigned the status of **Closed**. It is not recommended that you mess around with different statuses in this module as the module is looking for specific statuses to perform its process. After a business item is changed to Closed and when the next meeting is generated, that business item falls off the minutes automatically.

There are many times when a business item is discussed several weeks in a row without resolution. To accommodate for this, open the business item and add new comments to the top of the description field with a date. The description field will grow as each week you add some comments about what was discussed for this item.

Meeting Minutes is one of the several modules, where after the creation of the first meeting, creating the next meeting is quite simple. This module can even be used to prepare an agenda for next week's meeting. To create next week's meeting, open the previous meeting and select **Generate Meeting** from the **Select an Action** drop-down list. PCM will ask a few questions before it creates the next meeting with all the current unresolved business items already in the list. It also assumes that the same people will be in attendance at the meeting but this list can be adjusted.

Daily Reports

All seasoned superintendents record a daily diary of events on their projects. The daily report becomes the official daily diary of happenings for the project when an arbitrator wants to see how a project was built. Seasoned superintendents are very diligent in keeping this diary for themselves and for their organization. There are so many sections to a good daily report. The PCM sections are as follows:

- Comments
- Additional Comments
- Equipment
- Field Force
- Visitors
- Material Deliveries
- Schedule
- Weather

The following screenshot shows the **Daily Reports** module in PCM:

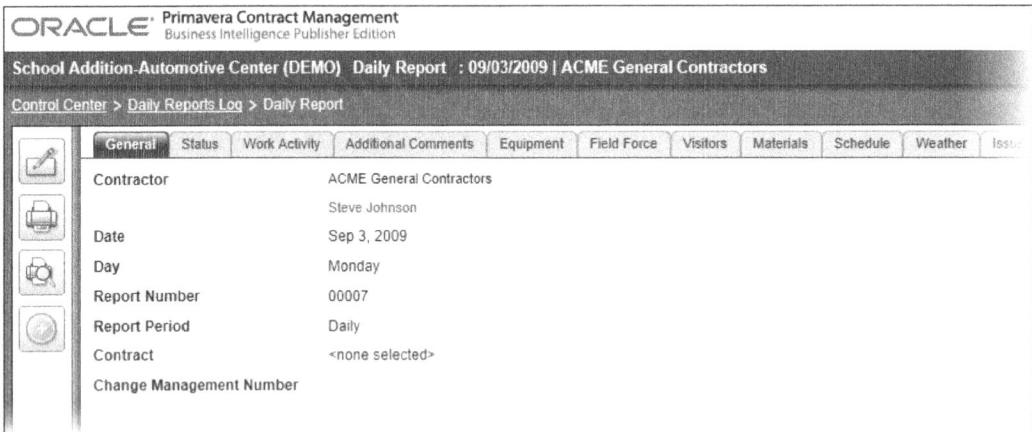

Each of these sections has many fields where information is stored about that particular day. Much of the information is also retrieved via drop-down lists to make it as easy and quick as possible. PCM also has the capability to lock the report by a manager so it is no longer editable.

Punch List

There is a need to record and manage the defects on the project prior to paying a contractor his final payment. At the end of a project or a phase of the project, there is a walk-through to review anything that needs fixing or is missing. Placing this information in PCM allows for assignment of **Ball In Court** and **Required Finish** date. With these pieces of information attached to each item that needs attention, reporting on the progress of the Punch List is very simple. The Punch List Items can also be monitored and displayed on the Control Center with the use of Alerts and Actions.

The Punch List Register lists all the items that need attention prior to final payment. These lists can be for your organization to accomplish or for your contractors to accomplish.

Summary

Keeping this information in one location with security and the ability to assign responsibility and required dates can streamline your ability to manage a project. This information compiled in this format can also keep you out of most litigation cases. The key is to be consistent on how the data is entered and the frequency of entering the data. You know the saying, "he who shows up to a litigation case with the largest, most organized pile of paper wins." PCM allows you to have a very large and very organized pile of electronic paper.

In the next chapter we will be looking at the out of the box connection of the Primavera products P6 and PCM. While this functionality is available, it is not what is expected of the project management community.

15
P6 and PCM

Most people believe that since P6 and PCM are both Oracle Primavera products, the integration between them should be perfect and seamless. It is not. While there is communication available between these two applications "out of the box," it is very rigid and not very user friendly. This chapter is dedicated to understanding what elements are available to these applications and how to best use this information.

Connecting the tools

For information to be available, the systems need connection information and login credentials. PCM has no concept of time and therefore it is very advantageous to connect these tools. Connecting the two adds an element of time to PCM and much more detailed contract information to P6. There is the capability to push and pull data from either tool. See the details in the following sections.

P6 connected to PCM

When P6 is connected to PCM, it means that P6 information is available to the PCM user. Once a P6 project is linked to an PCM project in the PCM setup, then most of the modules that have a schedule section will have a pick list of P6 activities in which to associate with that PCM record. There is nothing magical that happens. The **Schedule** tab information is a simple *get* of the P6 data *at that time* and populates that information in the PCM database. If any changes are made in P6 after this has been done, then nothing will change in PCM. It is a one-time *get* of the static information in P6. There is one exception to this; the **Schedule** module in PCM will display the schedule in real time. The other "sort-of" exception to this is in the submittal module. If a P6 schedule is linked to an PCM project and you use the **Successor Activity** field in the **Schedule** tab of the submittal, there is a button that allows you to *get* the current real-time data and repopulate the PCM fields to best manage your submittals. This is not dynamic, but it is available for each submittal.

All modules

Most of the modules used in PCM have a schedule tab where an activity can be selected from the P6 schedule and that data is pulled and stored in PCM. This data will be as of that time. As the schedule changes these values do *not* change. The following screenshot shows the **Schedule** tab of an RFI record. You can see the Activity ID as well as the Early Start and Early Finish dates from P6 populated in the RFI:

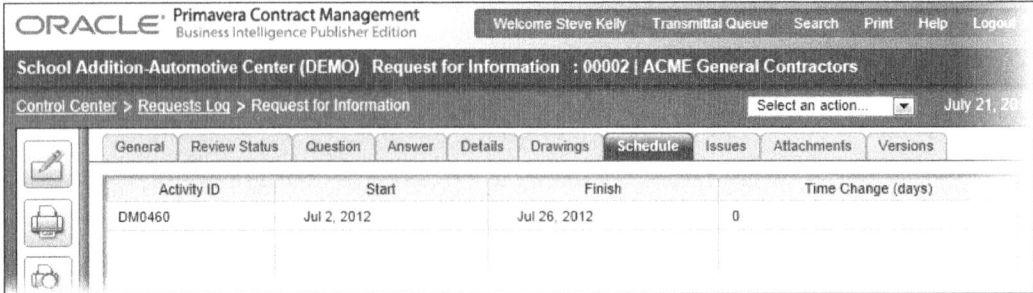

This feature only allows for one activity per record. There are also times where a schedule activity can be associated with a "child" record, such as a contract line item as shown in the following screenshot:

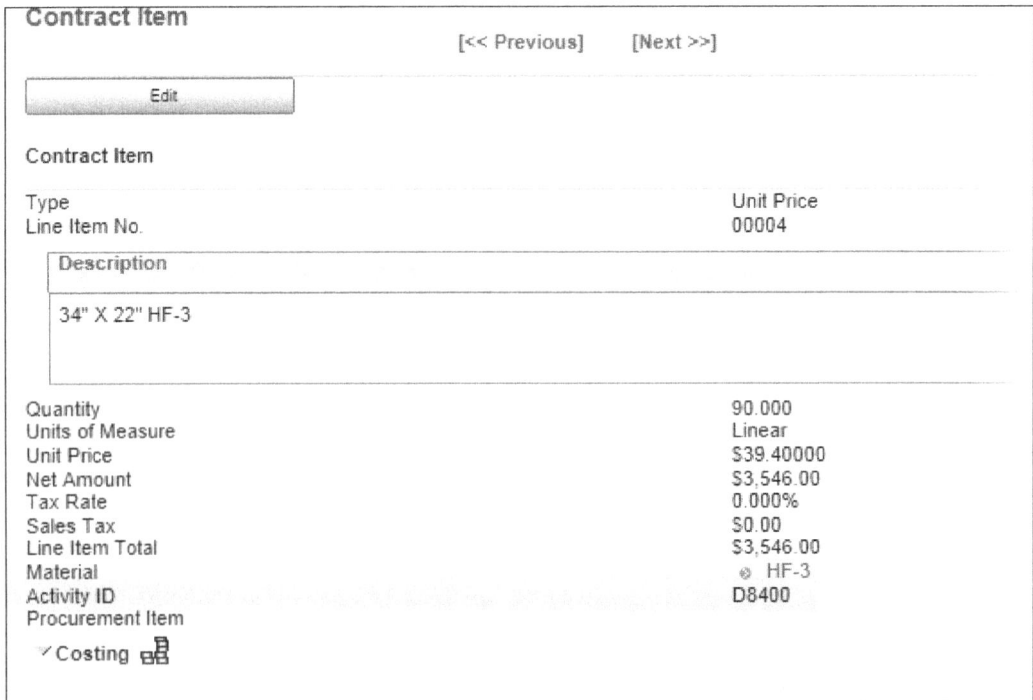

Other examples of modules where "child" records can be assigned an activity are:

- Meeting minute business items
- Punch list items
- All the monetary modules line items

Daily reports

The connection of the P6 schedule to PCM allows the user to use those activities in daily reports. When a P6 schedule is connected to a project then there is a link on the **Schedule** tab of the daily report named **Get Activities**. When this link is clicked, all the activities in the project that *should* be worked on that day will be listed in that tab. There is also the capability to add activities that were worked on that were not automatically pulled into the list, as shown in the following screenshot:

The capability also exists for the user of the daily report to progress these activities and have that information be pulled from PCM when you are in P6 (more on that later).

Submittals

The **Schedule** tab in submittals was briefly discussed. When this is properly used the fluidity of the schedule can be captured into PCM and vice versa. As the schedule and delivery of some items are key to the project coming in on time and budget, the capture of this flexibility is very important.

Payment requisitions

There can be a direct connection between the P6 schedule and individual line items of the payment requisition. Many owners will pay contractors based on schedule completion percent complete. When the P6 schedule is directly tied to pay items on the requisition, then the capability to press a button and have all the percent complete information be copied from schedule activities to the pay items is very powerful.

The following screenshot shows an activity assigned to each payment item:

PCM connected to P6

This may seem redundant, but it is very different. Just because you have connected P6 to PCM from within PCM does not mean that you can get PCM data while in P6. You need to make a connection to PCM from within P6 as well. This allows P6 to *get* information from PCM and populate specific P6 fields.

There are many areas that can be populated from PCM as shown in the following screenshot from P6:

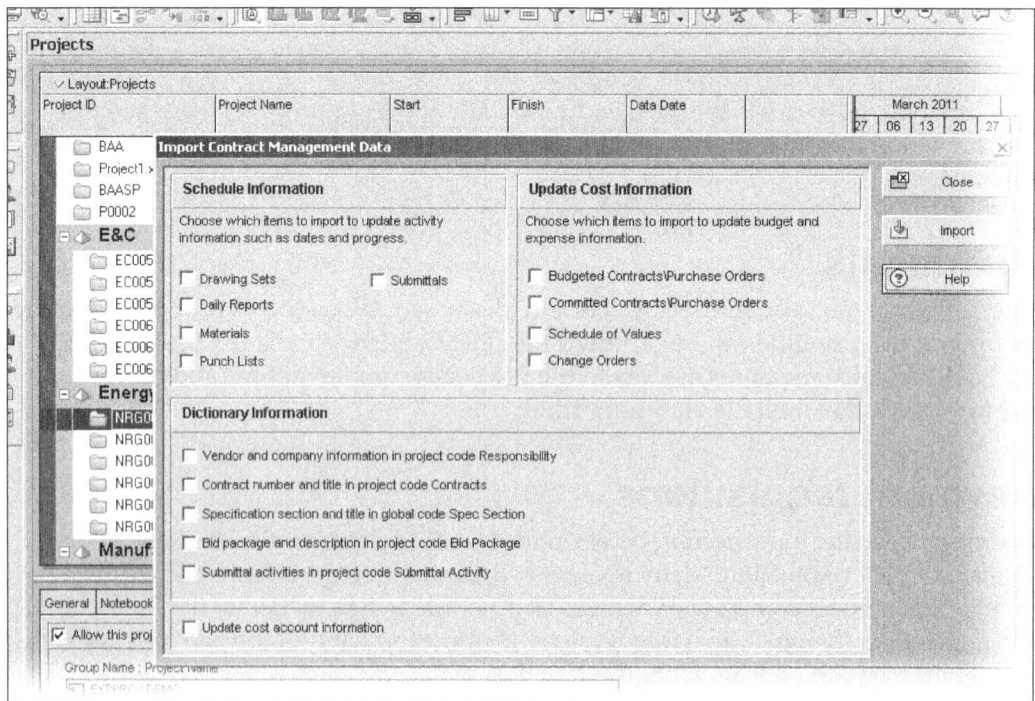

Schedule information

There are certain modules in PCM that P6 can draw from to get schedule or cost information, and update activities, dates, cost, and progress.

- **Drawing Set**: The Schedule tab of the drawing set is the information that P6 uses to update information. The checkboxes indicate that the activity has started.

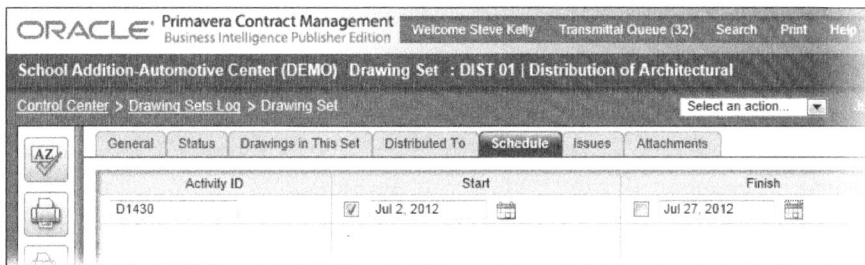

- **Daily Report**: This module allows for actual progressing the schedule from within PCM. This is not a real-time update, but the schedule activities for "today" can be retrieved to populate this list. Then the information can be entered into each activity for date started or finished, percent complete, and remaining duration. All this information can then be picked up by P6.

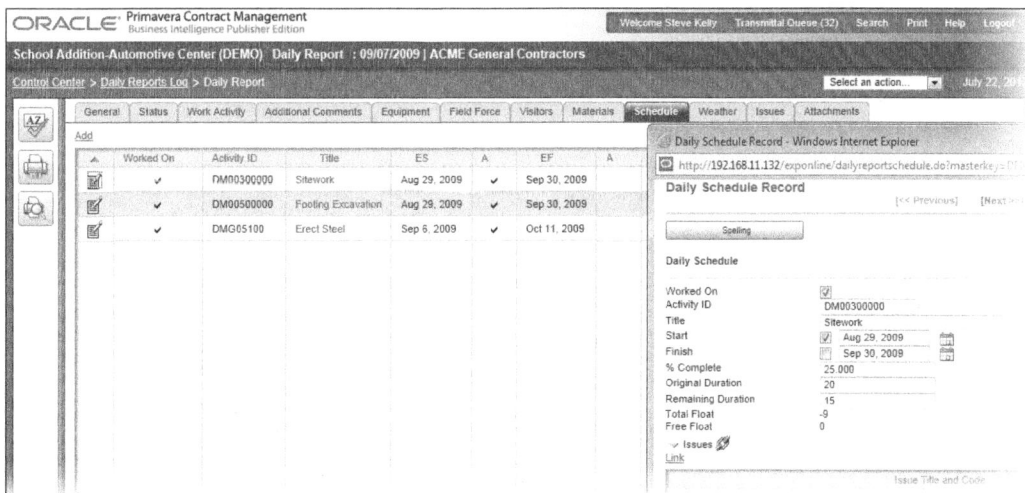

- **Materials Delivery**: The **Schedule** tab in the materials register can be populated with an activity and the dates can be adjusted to be pulled into P6.

> There are no checkboxes available for you to tell PCM that this activity has started or finished.

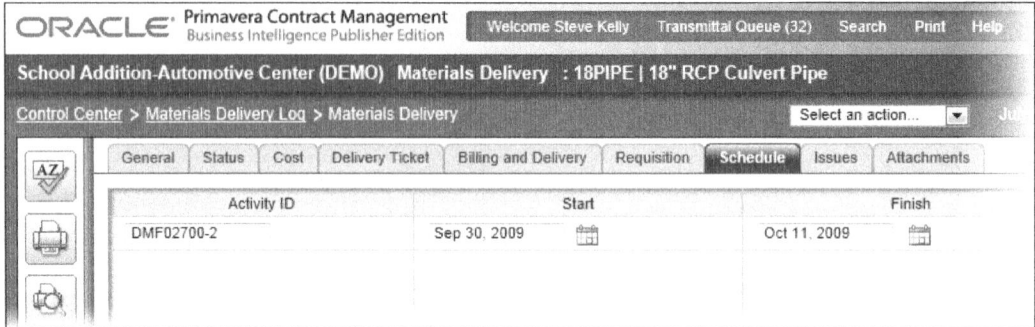

- **Punch Lists**: Each item in a punch list can be assigned an activity that can be edited for P6.

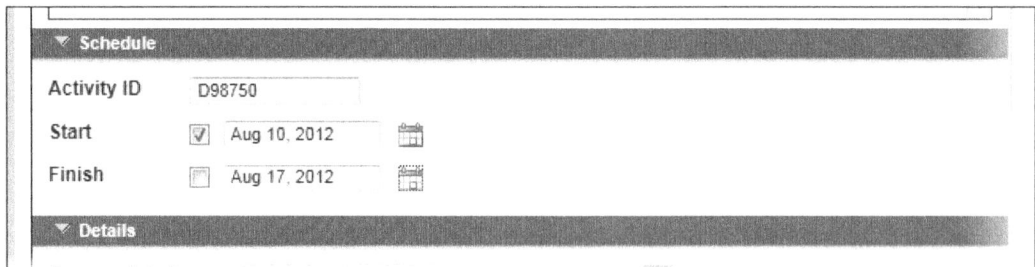

- **Submittal**: The **Schedule** tab of each submittal has a field called the **Successor Activity**. The information for this activity is pulled from P6. As the project progresses, you can click on the **Get Schedule Activity** link to get the most current P6 information for that activity.

All of these modules can provide P6 with information that changes the schedule. There are many schedulers that understandably do not want to allow another application to change the schedule. P6 does provide a text-based list of the activities it is about to change and the scheduler then is able to accept or reject the whole list. There is no selective picking of which activities he *does* or *does not* want the integration to affect.

Update cost information

The following four modules provide P6 with information to adjust cost and/or expense information. Like the previous section, the scheduler is given an opportunity to not allow all the activities to be affected.

- Budget contracts
- Commitment contracts and Purchase orders
- Payment requisitions
- Change orders

Dictionary information

You can synchronize several dictionaries that may be used in both tools. The following is a list of those dictionaries:

- **Vendor and company information**: This information is placed in a project code named `Responsibility`
- **Contract Numbers**: This information is placed in a project code called `Contracts`
- **Specification Sections**: This information in placed in a global code called `Spec Section`
- **Bid Package**: This information is placed in a project code called `Bid Package`
- **Submittal Activities**: This information is placed in a project code called `Submittal Activity`

The last checkbox is to integrate cost code information in PCM with the cost account field in P6. Any changes made in the PCM cost code list can be synchronized with P6.

Summary

While there are many places of integration between these two tools, it is also quite limiting and rigid to properly use this integration with any regularity. There are easy ways to integrate these tools using the **APIs** (**Application Programming Interface**) and/or web services. This allows for 100 percent flexibility in how these tools are integrated to match your business processes perfectly. There are many third-party developers that have expertise in this area.

The next chapter will discuss the road ahead and where you should go from here.

Where Do We Go from Here? 16

Believe it or not this book is a pretty high-level overview of PCM and the benefits you can glean from using it properly. Each module has its own set of unique characteristics that can be exploited. If all the modules worked the same then Oracle would have created one module that could be replicated and renamed. Some modules have money related to them while others are simple data entry modules. Almost every module could have its own book written about its characteristics and how to use them for your benefit.

One man's opinion

This information is presented to the reader from many years of experience and understanding of the capabilities of PCM as well as many years in the industry understanding the needs of the business. This is, however, one man's opinion on management and the usage of the system. There are many ways to use PCM. Every organization has its own processes and procedures to perform basically the same function. This opinion on the usage of PCM is, however, a great place to start and understand the modules and the thought processes required to use these modules.

The next step

Time to dive in. Take the information presented here and apply it to your own organization.

As was stated in the beginning, every organization is different and therefore will require some adjustments to the principles presented in these pages. Don't be afraid to play and see how this powerful system can be used to enhance how you perform your business operations. Do not try to eat the whole elephant in one bite. You will need to take a set of a few modules and see how they work for your organization. There are two basic types of modules in PCM, namely the **money modules** and the **document modules**. Look to implement one type first and not the whole application at one time; it will most likely fail and you will have unhappy users. That is just too much change in the organization to swallow. Consider implementing one or two modules that are easy to grasp, such as the **RFI** module. Using this module means you also turn on the **Companies** module as very little happens in PCM without having a company/contact involved. This will get the users to perform a task they are used to so they can get familiar with the system and how to enter data and move around the application.

No one likes change

If a survey of everyone in your office were taken, and they were asked one simple question: "Would you like it if we change how you do your job or keep things the way they are?" I think you know the answer; an overwhelming majority would prefer to keep the status quo. That is human nature. They most likely have had a bad experience with someone coming in and telling them that their life is going to get much better and easier with this "new" system. However, it turned out that after the tool was implemented, it was harder to do their jobs and for no foreseeable benefit (certainly not to their world).

Change for the sake of change is not what this is about. The object of implementing a tool like PCM is to provide a tool that helps them perform their jobs and/or provides an overall benefit to the organization that they did not already have. PCM is a tool for the office just like a circular saw is a tool for the carpenter. Can the carpenter cut that piece of wood without the electric circular saw? Of course he can, but that tool allows him to be more productive and efficient with his time. Can the project office manage changes, submittals, drawings, daily reports, and so on without PCM? Of course, it can. The object is to provide a tool that allows everyone to be more productive with their time. Even if they spend the same amount of time in their particular role, there is a benefit to the whole project and organization to have all aspects of the project in one centralized location for all those required to see.

Implementing PCM will not guarantee that all the roles will be done faster and better. It will just provide all the data in the same location with consistency of management across multiple projects. Most of the modules in PCM have been performed for centuries with various tools. Since you are entering all that information someplace, why not enter it into the "same" place or the same application?

Proper implementation

PCM is not a tool that can be loaded on your machine and you just start using it. Every time that method is tried, PCM gets a bad rap by users that don't understand how it works. It is a very *complex* tool and needs to be handled as such. You will need an implementation specialist that understands the tool extremely well and more importantly understands the business even better. It is a very configurable tool and can be wrapped around most business processes. Following is a suggested high-level implementation plan:

- **Establish business processes**: The business processes must be in place first. This is a tool that can reinforce business process but not create a business process. It is flexible enough to allow for some wiggle room within a process and yet rigid enough to require certain actions to be taken. That may all seam contradictory; however, it is a nice blend. Is PCM perfect? Absolutely not. Are there things that the PCM community really wishes that it would do? Absolutely. But like any other application of this magnitude, it cannot please everyone. It takes that seasoned implementation specialist to understand your business and best wrap the processes of the application around those processes. They can also help you to build processes if you are lacking in that area.

- **Win "buy-in" from the business**: If the business feels that a new system is being shoved down its throat then employees will most likely resist, and in some cases resist violently. The business must see benefit to them or at least to the organization for them to embrace the change in their world. During the design and testing of PCM, continue to receive feedback from the business so that they feel the tool and its configuration is theirs.

PCM can be very unforgiving. It will allow the users to go down the wrong road a long way before they figure out that it is the wrong road.

In concert with that issue, it will not just let you hop onto the right road; you must go all the way back to that fork in the road where you made the wrong choice and correct things there. That is what comes with the flexibility of the application. If a tool is too rigid and only allows for one way to perform a process, then it will not work for many businesses. All businesses are different.

The design for an application such as PCM is to have all forms of communication relating to your project in one place. This allows for searchability across all these records much quicker than trying to find that one letter or e-mail that was written months or years ago about a specific topic. PCM allows you to search all fields of all records within a project. It can search through those records much faster than you can search through file boxes in the back room someplace.

Proper training

Nobody likes to go to a three-day class and listen to the droning of an instructor who only knows a button to push but not why it needs to be pushed. Most computer application classroom training today is just that.

Even official Primavera training is for multiple days. The human mind just cannot soak in that much information and retain it for their benefit. How many times have you come back from a training course and said "Ok, I'm going to start using this program and use what I have learned". Five minutes after you sat down you start saying, "I know I saw the instructor do this, but I can't remember what they did."

Successful training is several two-to-four-hour time slots with each slot designed for a specific process and even perhaps for a specific role. It includes instruction from a person that can keep the training moving and fun and who has a deep understanding of the implementation process, the tools, and the business. Just having tool knowledge is not enough. The object of the training is to teach the "whys" of the process as well as the "how's". The students should learn *why* they are pushing that button or entering that field rather than just the *how*. Many times a field is being entered to benefit another process down the line or a completely different role. Without this understanding by the students, they feel like they are just trained monkeys being taught what buttons to push. Button-pushing training can be accomplished through screencasts or videos without the need of a qualified instructor. The instructor needs to be able to properly answer the *why* questions. Usage of training tools like the Oracle Universal Productivity Kit (UPK) is great to reinforce the classroom training. The classroom training allows for discussion and answering of questions.

Mentoring

Unfortunately, this step is usually left out or cut out by the project after training. This is a terrible mistake.

The mentoring process is the most important part of a complete implementation. You all know the saying, "You can lead a horse to water but you can't make it drink." The implementation process may provide some of the best tasting "water" and the training process can lead students right to the edge of the pond, but it is the mentoring process that will help them understand how good it tastes and they can taste it little bit at a time, most importantly, with someone else there to hold their hand. The next saying you all know is "misery loves company." As it was stated previously, no one likes change so this can be misery to most people. The mentoring process allows them to go through the change with someone that has been there and understands the frustrations and pains of change. Many times it is the same person as the trainer as this person is well known by the students and has hopefully gained their trust that he/she won't lead them astray and take them to places they don't want to go.

Summary

Information is king in this society; however, if you don't know how to manage this information or use it to your benefit then it becomes your enemy. Usually an organization does not understand this concept until it has been engaged in a lawsuit where if they had properly managed the documents and information they would have saved a lot of money. It has been said that if this system performs one task on a project, it keeps the organization out of court. If that is all it does then it is well worth the time and effort to use it well.

However, besides the documents, managing your project costs with this tool is so much easier and more informative than an accounting system. Accounting is great to tell you history, but it has no idea about the potential of your project. Let accounting pay the bills but let PCM allow you to manage your project and provide you with the information that you need to make proper and timely decisions. Now go out and have fun with this wonderful tool!!!

17

The New Contract
Management Tool

During the writing of this book there have been some significant changes from Primavera in relation to Contract Management. The Primavera Global Business Unit announced in July 2012 the purchase of a competitor's product called Skire. There was no immediate explanation as to the reason for this but it is now known. During the 2012 Oracle Open World in San Francisco it was announced that the Skire product, now named Primavera Unifier, will be the contract management tool of the future for Primavera. Let's look at what this means for the PCM community now and into the future. All the information in this chapter is as current as of the time of writing. There will certainly be more information that comes to light after the publishing of this book.

History

Primavera has known for many years that something had to be done with the PCM product. There are so many things that the community wanted it to do, that the list of enhancement requests was quite long. Many of these requests required major changes to the current core product. They knew that someday they would need to rewrite PCM from the ground up. It is this author's understanding (not verified) that this effort had already begun and would take one to two years to complete with a release of Version 1.0. Primavera had a decision to make; they could continue to develop a new product and wait for one to two years for a release with the anticipated response from the PCM community, or they could go and buy the technology and rebrand it as a Primavera product; they chose the latter. With the purchase of Skire, they claim that Unifier will solve over 70 percent of the current enhancement requests.

What does this mean?

This in no way changes any of the concepts and processes described in this book. The concepts of managing contracts remain the same regardless of which tool is used. As was said early on, PCM is simply a tool to be used to manage contracts in a centralized secure environment. The fact is that the look and feel of the tool delivered by Oracle Primavera does not change these concepts. Obviously, the screens will be different and some of the processes will change to match Unifier, but managing projects does not change just because the tool may be a bit different. While PCM was designed for the execution phase of a project, Unifier includes all the phases. This added functionality and the ability to manage all project phases will allow you to utilize one location for the management of a project before, during, and after the execution phase of the project. Primavera Unifier is simply the next major version of what we know as Contract Management with so much more.

What does Unifier do for you?

Skire Unifier has been a competitor of PCM for many years. There were many things that Unifier did that PCM could not do and was hard to sell against if you looked at features alone. When PCM won the bid, it was typically because of the ease of use and user friendliness. We are still not exactly sure what the Primavera Unifier tool will look like out of the box, but it is this author's understanding that it will have at least the functionality of the current PCM. The PCM community hopes for more. There are many features that Unifier provides that PCM has not had. Here are a few:

- Full project lifecycle management
  - ◦ Capital project and program management
  - ◦ Facilities management
  - ◦ Real estate management
  - ◦ Integrated workplace management
- Capital planning at the enterprise
- True funding and budgeting
- Cash flow management
- Internal workflow engine
- Much more configurable interface
- More robust Cost Worksheet
- Good e-mail integration
- Mobile capabilities

Oracle has broken the Unifier product into five deliverable pieces, each with its own license and cost:

- **Primavera Capital Planning** replaces Primavera OPPM for Portfolio Management
- **Primavera Project Delivery Management** replaces PCM non-cost related functionality
- **Primavera Cost Controls** replaces PCM and partner cost related functionality
- **Primavera Facility Management** is a new application to support work order and facility management
- **Primavera Real Estate Management** is a new application to support real estate (rentals) management

To provide the same functionality as the current PCM product an organization will need to purchase two components:

1. Project Delivery
2. Cost Controls

With these features and levels of management, Unifier takes PCM to the next level. With the base Unifier product being a platform, the system can truly be configured to the business model of the customer. Out of the box, Unifier will be configured for contract management with workflows and entry forms predesigned; however, the "platform" itself will not be available to purchase.

The following screenshot is the original login screen for Primavera Unifier:

It is the ultimate goal of Primavera to incorporate many of its products into the Unifier platform. P6 is planned to be incorporated soon as well as several others. This will bring the Primavera products under one umbrella, which is what Primavera has been trying to do for years. This will also bring administration, reporting, workflow, integration, and more under one application as a unified approach.

The following two screenshots were provided by Oracle as part of a presentation to the user community of what is coming in the future relating to Skire, which includes Contracts and Scheduling under one application:

The following screenshot is another look at the new Unifier as it was presented at the time.

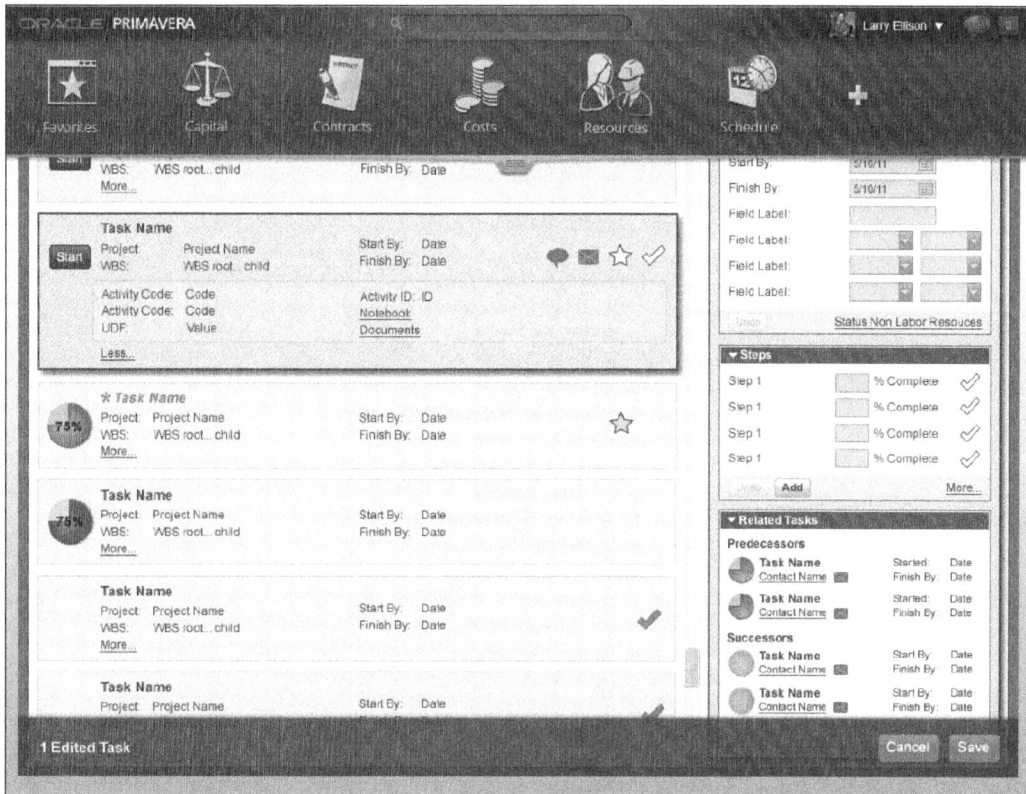

The following screenshot seems to be the layout of the Project Delivery modules within Unifier that map similarly to the folders and modules in the current PCM.

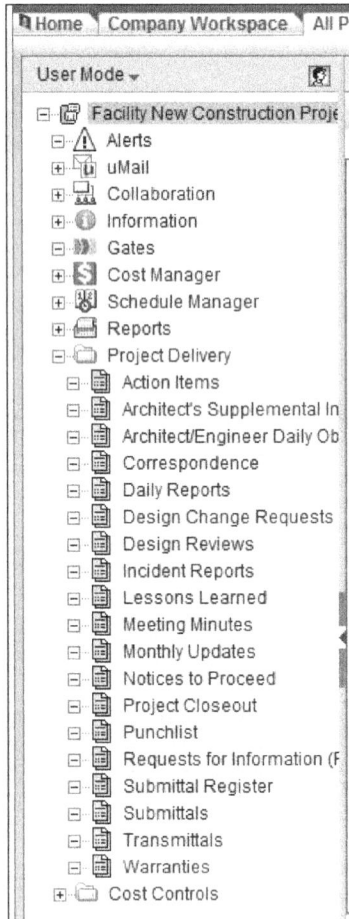

The following screenshot shows the Cost Modules in Unifier that map to similar modules in PCM.

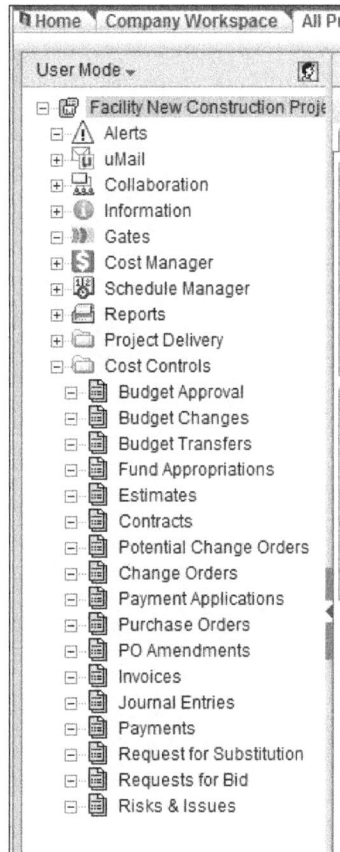

Much more information is yet to come. The information is being released by Oracle as it becomes available. There is no information related to the timing other than the "near future."

Summary

Whether you are using the existing PCM or the new Unifier, managing contracts and the data that a project collects is the ultimate goal. Using either of these tools allows you to have one secure location for all your project communication and project costs, which allow you to make timely and accurate decisions.

These systems allow you to keep as many fires from starting as possible, which means fewer fires to put out during the course of the project.

> *"Even if you put a fire out quickly there is still residue that needs cleaning up."*

To keep up with the latest developments of Primavera Unifier, follow this author's blog at www.promanagementsystems.com/blog.

Index

[PACKT] PUBLISHING   enterprise ✺
professional expertise distilled

Thank you for buying
Oracle Primavera Contract Management, Business Intelligence Publisher Edition v14

About Packt Publishing

Packt, pronounced 'packed', published its first book "Mastering phpMyAdmin for Effective MySQL Management" in April 2004 and subsequently continued to specialize in publishing highly focused books on specific technologies and solutions.

Our books and publications share the experiences of your fellow IT professionals in adapting and customizing today's systems, applications, and frameworks. Our solution based books give you the knowledge and power to customize the software and technologies you're using to get the job done. Packt books are more specific and less general than the IT books you have seen in the past. Our unique business model allows us to bring you more focused information, giving you more of what you need to know, and less of what you don't.

Packt is a modern, yet unique publishing company, which focuses on producing quality, cutting-edge books for communities of developers, administrators, and newbies alike. For more information, please visit our website: www.packtpub.com.

About Packt Enterprise

In 2010, Packt launched two new brands, Packt Enterprise and Packt Open Source, in order to continue its focus on specialization. This book is part of the Packt Enterprise brand, home to books published on enterprise software – software created by major vendors, including (but not limited to) IBM, Microsoft and Oracle, often for use in other corporations. Its titles will offer information relevant to a range of users of this software, including administrators, developers, architects, and end users.

Writing for Packt

We welcome all inquiries from people who are interested in authoring. Book proposals should be sent to author@packtpub.com. If your book idea is still at an early stage and you would like to discuss it first before writing a formal book proposal, contact us; one of our commissioning editors will get in touch with you.

We're not just looking for published authors; if you have strong technical skills but no writing experience, our experienced editors can help you develop a writing career, or simply get some additional reward for your expertise.

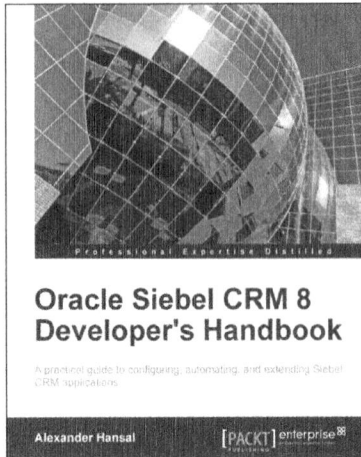

Oracle Siebel CRM 8 Developer's Handbook

ISBN: 978-1-84968-186-5   Paperback: 576 pages

A practical guide to configuring automating, and extending Siebel CRM applications

1. Use Siebel Tools to configure and automate Siebel CRM applications

2. Understand the Siebel Repository and its object types

3. Configure the Siebel CRM user interface – applets, views, and screens

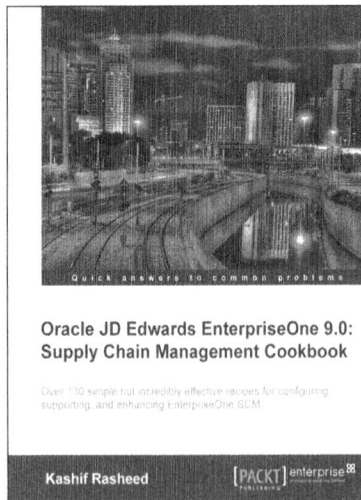

Oracle JD Edwards EnterpriseOne 9.0: Supply Chain Management Cookbook

ISBN: 978-1-84968-196-4   Paperback: 370 pages

Over 130 simple but incredibly effective receipes for configuring, supporting, and enhancing EnterpriseOne SCM

1. Master all that the EnterpriseOne SCM modules have to offer with this book and e-book full of step by step instructions

2. Go deeper into SCM functionality with special orders and approvals

3. This recipe-based guide packed with images, and concluding with a real-world Supply Chain blueprint, helps you fully absorb each step by step tas

Please check **www.PacktPub.com** for information on our titles

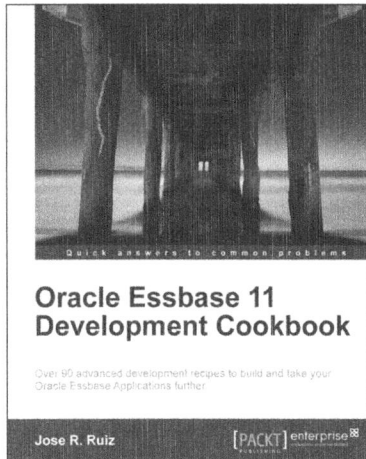

Oracle Essbase 11 Development Cookbook

ISBN: 978-1-84968-326-5   Paperback: 400 pages

Over 90 advanced development recipes to build and take your Oracle Essbase Applications further

1. This book and e-book will provide you with the tools needed to successfully build and deploy your Essbase application

2. Includes the major components that need to be considered when designing an Essbase application

3. This book can be used to build calculations, design process automation, add security, integrate data, and report off an Essbase cube

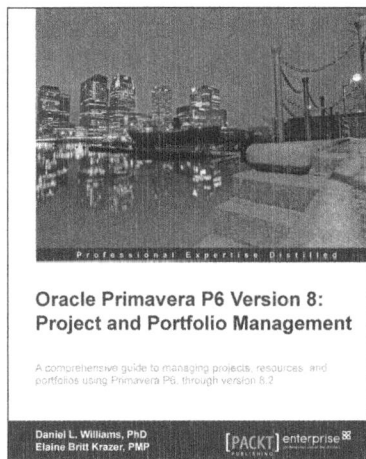

Oracle Primavera P6 Version 8: Project and Portfolio Management

ISBN: 978-1-84968-468-2   Paperback: 348 pages

A comprehensive guide to managing projects, resources, and portfolios using Primavera P6, through version 8.2

1. Get a detailed overview of Oracle Primavera P6 Enterprise Project Portfolio Management.

2. Manage your projects from just anywhere using simple e-mail and the P6 iPhone app.

3. Learn to create a new project in the P6 Professional Client

CPSIA information can be obtained at www.ICGtesting.com
Printed in the USA
LVOW020642141212

311621LV00004B/111/P

9 781849 686907